INTO THE WARDROBE

INTO THE WARDROBE

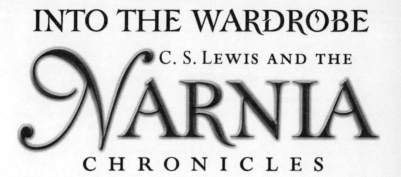

C. S. LEWIS AND THE

NARNIA

CHRONICLES

David C. Downing

JB JOSSEY-BASS
A Wiley Imprint
www.josseybass.com

Jossey-Bass books and products are available through most bookstores. To contact Jossey-Bass
directly call our Customer Care Department within the U.S. at 800-956-7739, outside the
U.S. at 317-572-3986, or fax 317-572-4002.

Jossey-Bass also publishes its books in a variety of electronic formats. Some content that
appears in print may not be available in electronic books.

Library of Congress Cataloging-in-Publication Data

Downing, David C.
  Into the wardrobe: C.S. Lewis and the Narnia chronicles / David C. Downing.—1st ed.
    p. cm.
  Includes bibliographical references and index.
  ISBN-13: 978-0-7879-7890-7 (alk. paper)
  ISBN-10: 0-7879-7890-6 (alk. paper)
  1. Lewis, C. S. (Clive Staples), 1898–1963. Chronicles of Narnia. 2. Children's stories,
English—History and criticism. 3. Christian fiction, English—History and criticism.
4. Fantasy fiction, English—History and criticism. 5. Narnia (Imaginary place) I. Title.
PR6023.E926C5327 2005
823'.912—dc22   2005013177

Printed in the United States of America

FIRST EDITION
HB Printing   10 9 8 7 6 5 4 3 2 1

CONTENTS

For friends and fellow scholars
who have gone into the Wardrobe before me:
Colin Duriez, Paul F. Ford, Walter Hooper,
and Peter J. Schakel

A C. S. LEWIS TIME LINE

1894	Marriage of Albert Lewis and Florence ("Flora") Hamilton.
1895	June 16: Birth of Warren Hamilton Lewis.
1898	November 29: Birth of Clive Staples Lewis.
1905	Lewis family moves into a new house, Little Lea.
1908	August 23: Death of Flora Lewis.
	September: Lewis travels to Wynyard School in Watford, England.
1910	Lewis spends the fall term at Campbell College in Belfast.
1911	Lewis enrolls at Cherbourg House in Malvern, England. He gives up his childhood faith.
1913	Lewis begins studies at Malvern College in Malvern.
1914	Lewis is privately tutored by William T. Kirkpatrick until March 1917.
1917	April: Lewis matriculates at University College, Oxford.
	June: Lewis enlists in the British army. He meets E.F.C. "Paddy" Moore; his mother, Janie Moore; and his sister Maureen.
	November: Lewis arrives in the trenches of France on his nineteenth birthday.

1918   April: Lewis wounded in action; Paddy Moore is reported missing in action in March and confirmed dead in August.

1919   January: Lewis returns to his studies in Oxford. Publication of *Spirits in Bondage,* a cycle of poems, under the name Clive Hamilton. Lewis moves in with Mrs. Moore and Maureen.

1920–1923   Lewis earns Firsts in classics, philosophy, and English.

1925   Lewis elected a Fellow of Magdalen College, Oxford.

1926   *Dymer,* a narrative poem.
     Lewis first meets J.R.R. Tolkien.

1929   Lewis reluctantly embraces theism. Death of Albert Lewis.

1930   Lewis and the Moores move to the Kilns, just north of Oxford.

1931   Lewis re-embraces Christianity, soon after a late-night talk with J.R.R. Tolkien.

1932   Warren Lewis retires from the British army and moves to the Kilns.

1933   *The Pilgrim's Regress,* an allegorical account of Lewis's spiritual journey.
     Meetings of Lewis and his circle of friends are dubbed "the Inklings."

1936   *The Allegory of Love,* a scholarly study of allegorical love poetry.

1938   *Out of the Silent Planet,* first book of the Space Trilogy.

1939	World War II begins. Evacuated children arrive at the Kilns.
	Rehabilitations and Other Essays, a collection of literary appreciations.
1940	*The Problem of Pain,* a Christian meditation on suffering.
1941	Lewis gives his first series of radio talks for the British Broadcasting Corporation (BBC).
1942	*A Preface to Paradise Lost.*
	The Screwtape Letters, fanciful correspondence between a senior devil and an apprentice tempter.
	Lewis gives two more series of BBC radio talks.
1943	*Perelandra,* the second book of the Space Trilogy.
	The Abolition of Man, a critique of contemporary culture.
1944	Lewis gives a fourth series of talks on BBC radio.
1945	*That Hideous Strength,* the final book of the Space Trilogy.
1946	*The Great Divorce,* a fantasy about denizens of hell who are allowed to visit heaven.
1947	*Miracles,* a philosophical defense of supernaturalism.
1948	Lewis elected a Fellow of the Royal Society of Literature.
1950	*The Lion, the Witch and the Wardrobe.*
1951	*Prince Caspian: The Return to Narnia.*
	Mrs. Moore dies.

1952   *Mere Christianity.*
        The Voyage of the "Dawn Treader."
        Lewis first meets Joy Davidman Gresham in
        person, after a lively two-year correspondence.
1953   *The Silver Chair.*
1954   *English Literature in the Sixteenth Century, Excluding
        Drama,* volume 3 of the *Oxford History of English
        Literature.*
        Lewis accepts the Chair of Medieval and
        Renaissance English at Cambridge University.
        The Horse and His Boy.
1955   *The Magician's Nephew.*
        Surprised by Joy, a memoir of Lewis's early life
        and his return to faith.
1956   Lewis marries Joy Davidman Gresham in a civil
        ceremony; later in the year, Joy is diagnosed
        with cancer.
        The Last Battle.
        Till We Have Faces, a novel based on the Cupid
        and Psyche myth.
1957   Lewis marries Joy in an Anglican ceremony.
1958   *Reflections on the Psalms.*
1960   *The Four Loves.*
        Joy Davidman Gresham Lewis dies.
1961   *A Grief Observed,* published originally under the
        pen name N. W. Clerk.
        An Experiment in Criticism.
1962   Lewis writes *The Discarded Image,* an exposition
        of the medieval worldview, which was published
        posthumously in 1964.

1963   Lewis writes *Letters to Malcolm: Chiefly on Prayer,*
            which was also published posthumously in
            1964.
            November 22: Death of C. S. Lewis, one week
            short of his sixty-fifth birthday.

INTRODUCTION

The Child as Father of the Man

One of C. S. Lewis's closest friends in later years, the poet Ruth
Pitter, observed that his response to daily life reflected "an
almost uniquely persisting *child's* sense of glory and nightmare."
At first glance, this seems an unlikely description of one of the
most distinguished and widely known professors of English at
Oxford during the 1930s and 1940s. Apart from his fame as a
lecturer, Lewis was the author of the dauntingly erudite *Allegory
of Love,* the "diabolically clever" *Screwtape Letters,* and the pene-
trating cultural critique *The Abolition of Man.* Yet Pitter's impres-
sion is confirmed by many others who knew Lewis at the time.
He loved Milton's *Paradise Lost* (and could quote it from memory), but he also cherished the stories of Beatrix Potter. In his
books, he might illustrate a point by citing a medieval theologian who wrote in Latin, or he might quote instead from *The
Wind in the Willows.*

Source materials are listed in the Notes at the end of this volume, arranged
by page number and key words.

Some of his contemporaries were shocked when the eminent C. S. Lewis started writing children's stories. Even before he became known as the author of the now-classic Chronicles of Narnia, he had already put together one of the most remarkable writing careers of the twentieth century. He is still acknowledged as one of leading literary scholars of his generation, having composed a volume for the prestigious *Oxford History of English Literature* and written books on medieval literature, Milton, and Spenser, all of which continue to be highly regarded by specialists in English. He has also garnered worldwide recognition for his writings on Christian faith and practice. *The Screwtape Letters* (1942) became an international best-seller and landed his face on the cover of *Time* magazine (Sept. 8, 1947). Lewis's "Broadcast Talks" on Christianity for the British Broadcasting Corporation during World War II, later published as *Mere Christianity,* made his voice (after Churchill's) the most recognized in Britain.

Clearly, Lewis had already built a formidable reputation as a critic, scholar, and Christian apologist before he ever turned his hand to children's stories. He wrote his Narnia books in his leisure hours after his "serious" work of the day, usually composing only one draft and making minor revisions. Yet the Narnia chronicles have been hailed in *The Oxford Companion to Children's Literature* as "the most sustained achievement in fantasy for children by a 20th-century author." And they have been perennial best-sellers as well; they are currently purchased at a rate of more than a million copies a year.

Lewis once commented that "humanity does not pass through phases as a train passes through stations: being alive, it has the privilege of always moving yet never leaving anything behind. Whatever we have been, in some sort we still are." This is nowhere more true than in his own Chronicles of Narnia. When Lewis took up children's fiction, he did not cease to be Lewis the Christian, Lewis the medieval and Renaissance scholar, or Lewis the literary artist. Perhaps less consciously, he also did not leave behind a number of his own childhood experiences, particularly the untimely death of his mother and his traumatic years in English boarding schools.

Unlike his good friend J.R.R. Tolkien, Lewis did not publish children's stories that had started out as tales he spun for his own sons and daughters. Lewis was a bachelor when he wrote the Narnia chronicles and had no children of his own. He confessed that he was generally uncomfortable around children, a trait he considered a character flaw. This makes it all the more intriguing how Lewis could capture so unforgettably the mindset of young people and how he could conjure up the kind of adventures in which they take such delight.

One of Lewis's biographers, A. N. Wilson, answers this question by saying Lewis wrote the Narnia chronicles for "the child who was within himself." Though references to one's inner child have become tiresome in recent years, Lewis would probably have agreed. After all, it was Lewis who wrote to a child with the delightful name of Phyllida, "I don't think age matters so much as people think. Parts of me are still 12 and I think other parts were already 50 when I was 12." This simple comment may explain the unique narrating voice in the chronicles: it sounds like the part of Lewis who is fifty writing for the part of him who is still twelve.

In a similar vein, Lewis commented that "youth and age only touch the surface of our lives." Whether or not this is true in most cases, it was certainly true of him. Echoing what Ruth Pitter said about Lewis's childlike sense of glory and nightmare, another friend, Kathleen Raines, said he had about him an aura of "boyish greatness." Lewis would not have been offended by such a remark. He considered the willingness to become like a child a mark of maturity. "When I became a man," he explained, "I put away childish things, including the fear of childishness and the desire to be very grown up."

Paradoxically, Lewis's stories for children are also the products of his maturity. The mellow spirituality of the chronicles makes some of Lewis's earlier fiction, such as *The Pilgrim's Regress* (1933), seem rather shrill and heavy-handed by comparison. And the effortless, musical prose of the Narnia stories easily surpasses in literary artistry the poems Lewis labored over so diligently in his youth.

In accepting the constraints of writing children's fiction, Lewis was actually able to pour more of his whole self into his writing, including his love of wonder and enchantment, his affection for animals and homespun things, his shrewd observations about human nature, his vast reading, and his robust humor, not to mention theological speculations, medieval scholarship, and arcane linguistic jokes.

The thirteenth-century theologian Thomas Aquinas articulated his entire worldview and philosophy of life in his weighty and laborious *Summa Theologica*. It can be argued that Lewis offered his *Summa* in the sprightly and spontaneous chronicles. Of his more than fifty books, these stories are widely considered the ones that will most ensure for Lewis an enduring literary legacy. The Narnia stories are well-paced and engaging, a reliable source of refreshment and delight. But beneath their deceptively simple surface, the chronicles also provide richly textured narratives of unexpected depth.

Each Narnia book is like a little wardrobe. It contains a looking glass in which readers will see themselves in surprising new ways. And when they turn the pages, they enter a place of wonder, a visionary world of bustling vitality, sparkling beauty, and spiritual clarity.

CHAPTER ONE

The Life of C. S. Lewis

The Chronicles of Narnia were published at the rate of one per year, beginning in 1950 and ending in 1956. Writing seven books in seven years sounds like a remarkable accomplishment, but actually, Lewis was far more productive than that. The Narnia stories were released one per year to maximize sales, the way big-budget film series are released nowadays. But Lewis managed to complete all seven books between 1948 and 1954, while fulfilling his responsibilities as an Oxford don and working steadily on his scholarly tome *English Literature in the Sixteenth Century, Excluding Drama* (1954), and his memoir *Surprised by Joy* (1955).

Of course, to say the books were created in the late 1940s and early 1950s is to speak of the writing process, not the creative process as a whole. While the Narnia chronicles were written at a pace of one per year, they were most of Lewis's lifetime in the making. Virtually every year of his life from early childhood on contributed major strands or minute threads to the complex tapestry that would become the Narnia stories.

Childhood in the North of Ireland

C. S. Lewis is widely recognized for his careful observation and his careful selection of words. Both these traits emerged early in his career—by the age of four. When he was about three, his mother bought him a toy train engine, and the store clerk offered to tie a string on the front. Young Lewis, then called simply "Baby," strenuously objected: "Baby doesn't see any string on the engines Baby sees in the station." Not long after this incident, the little boy decided he didn't want to be called Baby anymore, nor any of its variations such as Babs, Babsie, or Babbins. He marched up to his mother, pointed to himself, and declared, "He is Jacksie," refusing to answer to any other name. And so Jacksie, later shortened to Jack, he became to his friends and family for the rest of his life.

Clive Staples Lewis was born in Belfast in 1898, the second son of Albert Lewis, a successful Belfast attorney, and Florence Hamilton Lewis. Descended from Welsh farmers and mechanics, Albert was one of the first of his family to complete a college education and enter a profession. He was known for his eloquence as a speaker and debater, a man with a phenomenal memory who loved to quote freely from his favorite works of literature.

Florence Hamilton, who preferred to be called Flora, was descended from more aristocratic stock. Her father was a rector in the Church of Ireland (Anglican), and his forebears included a number of high officials in the Church. Flora's mother's family, the Warrens, could trace their ancestry to a Norman knight buried in Battle Abbey in Sussex. Flora was one of the first women to graduate from Queen's College in Belfast, taking a first-class degree in logic and a second-class degree in mathematics.

Both Albert and Flora were avid readers, and both tried their hand at creative writing. Albert wrote adventure yarns with titles such as "James's Adventure," "The Runaway Boy," and "Frank Fearless." None of these stories ever found their way into print. Flora was more successful; her tale called "The Princess Rosetta" was published in 1889 by a magazine in London called *The Household Journal*.

Albert Lewis and Flora Hamilton were married in 1894. Their first son, Warren Hamilton Lewis, was born the following year, christened with the surnames of his mother's parents. Clive Staples was born three years later, on November 29, 1898. Though Clive and Staples were also respected names from Flora's side of the family, her second son went straight from Baby to Jack, seldom using his given names.

In 1905, the Lewis family moved from a modest semi-detached villa to their new house, called Little Lea, in a fashionable suburb overlooking the Belfast Lough. In later years, Lewis would describe this big rambling structure as "almost a major character" in his life story, a place "of long corridors, empty sunlit rooms, upstairs indoor silences [and] attics explored in solitude." His brother Warren recalled that these attics often consisted of long tunnel-like spaces that children could use as secret passageways, entering through a small door in one room and coming out another. Though this space was largely wasted in Little Lea, it certainly was not wasted in Lewis's imagination, for he used such an attic in *The Magician's Nephew* to send Digory and Polly not just into new rooms but into new worlds.

One of the Lewis cousins, Claire Clapperton, also recalled a large, ornately carved oak wardrobe, which had been built by Albert's father, at Little Lea. Claire remembered that sometimes as children they would climb into the wardrobe and sit in the dark, listening to "Jacks" tell adventure stories. (This wardrobe is now on display at the Marion E. Wade Center at Wheaton College in Wheaton, Illinois.)

C. S. Lewis described his brother Warren as one of the great blessings of his childhood, someone who helped shape the way Lewis defined himself in relation to the world. "Warnie," or "Badger," and Jack spent many a rainy afternoon poring over the books in their parents' overflowing library, delighting especially in children's stories by Edith Nesbit and Beatrix Potter, as well as tales about "knights-in-armor" and "dressed animals." They also created their own imaginary worlds of "India" and "Animal-Land," which they later combined into the kingdom of Boxen.

Young Lewis sometimes wrote about chivalrous mice or rabbits who rode out in full armor to do battle with cats. But most of the Boxen tales focus on parliamentarian maneuvers and polite small talk among members of the privileged classes. Lewis would later pronounce his childhood creations to be "astonishingly prosaic" because they contained so much routine grown-up conversation, with hardly a trace of mystery or magic. It seems one of those quirks of human nature that Albert Lewis, whose life revolved around politics and practical legal matters, should write exotic stories of far-flung adventure. But when his young son Jack, who steeped himself in works of fantasy and imagination, turned to fiction, he wrote about political wrangles and humdrum civic affairs.

The Lewis brothers grew up during the time of "the troubles" in Ireland, tensions between Catholics and Protestants that have yet to be fully resolved. Lewis's father Albert was a stout Ulsterman,
vigorously defending the rights of the Protestants in the north of Ireland. His mother, though also Protestant, tried to stress cooperation and peaceful coexistence. Despite these background tensions, Lewis generally recalled his early childhood as a time of loving parents, good food, and plenty of room for outdoor play, as well as the special blessing of a beloved nurse, Lizzie Endicott.

Lizzie was warm and effervescent, entertaining the boys with Irish folktales of leprechauns, lost pots of gold, and voyages to mystic isles. In *Surprised by Joy,* Lewis described Lizzie Endicott with unabashed nostalgia and affection, saying that "even the exacting memory of childhood can discover no flaw— nothing but kindness, gaiety, and good sense," concluding that she was "as nearly as a human can be, simply good." Lewis's fond recollection of his childhood nurse reveals how many of his lifelong attitudes were shaped in these early years. Throughout his many books, the words *nurse* and *nursery* virtually always connote that which is simple but also that which is true and good. For example, he warns in his essay "The Poison of Subjectivism," "Unless we return to the crude and nursery-like belief in objective values, we perish." In *Prince Caspian,* the young prince learns about Aslan and the true history of Narnia from "the person he loved best," his nurse. And in *The Voyage of the "Dawn Treader,"* the intrepid mouse Reepicheep discovers that the nursery rhyme about the "utter East" he learned in his cradle turns out to be quite an accurate prophecy of what to expect as one approaches Aslan's country by sea.

One of the highlights of the year for the Lewis brothers was their summer holiday on the Irish shore with their mother. Among the sites Lewis remembered visiting as a boy was Dunluce Castle on the north coast, an impressive ruin overlooking the Atlantic Ocean. When he was about eight years old, Lewis drew a charming and surprisingly sure-handed picture of a castle by the sea, which resembles Dunluce both in its shape and its position on a rocky promontory. The same castle may have contributed something many years later to Lewis's mental image of Cair Paravel, the seat of the kings and queens of Narnia.

Throughout the years, Lewis always associated his childhood with a happy and secure home, the simple goodness of a beloved nurse, and the freedom to roam through empires of imagination with his brother Warren. And in Lewis's books, the words *child* and *childhood,* sometimes even *childish,* tend to carry the same connotations—simplicity, self-forgetfulness, imagination, and wonder. In discussing classical literature, Lewis quotes approvingly a scholar who says that a child reading Homer in translation for love of the story may be "nearer by twenty centuries to the old Greeks" than a trained scholar because he is "not grubbing for beauties but pressing the siege." In *The Problem of Pain,* Lewis comments that in spiritual matters, "the learned and the adult have no advantage at all over the simple and the child," explaining that "from our own childhood we remember that before our elders thought us capable of understanding anything, we already had spiritual experiences as pure and as momentous as any we have undergone since."

The pure and momentous experiences Lewis has in mind here are the recurrences of *Joy,* his word for *Sehnsucht,* the longing for some lost paradise that is itself a kind of paradise to feel. In *Surprised by Joy,* Lewis recalls one summer day when he was only six that there arose in him a memory of an earlier time when his brother had made a toy garden, bits of twigs and moss arranged in a biscuit tin. Lewis compares the momentary sensation that came with this memory to John Milton's "enormous bliss" of Eden, saying that this was his first experience of beauty.

Later, in reading Beatrix Potter's *Squirrel Nutkin,* the young Lewis again experienced a nameless longing, an "unsatisfied desire which is itself more desirable than any other satisfaction." There was always something elusive in this desire. In looking at pictures of autumn leaves in *Squirrel Nutkin,* he longed for the real trees outside his house, for the robust aromas and the crisp leaves crackling under his feet. But then walking among the actual trees in autumn made him long for the pictures he had seen in the book.

Lewis reports a third visitation of Joy when he was reading a Longfellow translation of Nordic myths and legends and came across these lines:

> *I heard a voice that cried,*
> *Balder the beautiful*
> *Is dead, is dead—*

Although he had no idea at the time who Balder was, these lines filled him with the particular kind of Joy he called *Northernness,* a solemn vision of things "cold, spacious, severe, pale, and remote."

Of course, nature itself could also be a direct source of Joy for the young Lewis. From the front door of Little Lea, Jack and Warren could look out beyond bustling Belfast and see a low line of distant hills across the lough, seeming to float in cool serenity above the dust and noise of the city. Looking back, Lewis would say that gazing at those hills created in him a life-long yearning for unreachable horizons.

From an Idyllic Childhood to a Traumatic Boyhood

For Lewis, childhood came to an abrupt end at the age of nine when his mother died. She was diagnosed with cancer early in 1908 and passed away within six months, at the age of forty-six. That was a harrowing time for the whole Lewis family, and for Warren and Jack, the period of decline was no less traumatic than the death itself. For the boys, the bereavement began several months before the death, as their mother was withdrawn from them into the hands of doctors and nurses, while the house became a place of alien medicinal smells, late-night footsteps in the hallway, and whispered conversations.

Besides losing his mother, Jack in a very real sense lost his father and his home as well. Even before the onset of Flora's illness, young Jack had described his father in a little daybook as a man with a "bad temper, very sensible, nice when not in a bad temper." Lewis felt that his father never fully recovered from the loss of his wife. He had always been a highly emotional man, and this great sorrow made him behave unpredictably, sometimes lashing out at his sons for no good reason. Lewis would later conclude that during these months, Albert unfortunately lost his sons nearly as completely as he lost his wife. The anguished time of Flora's decline and death set a pattern of strained relations between Jack and his father that would persist for over two decades, until 1929, when Albert fell into his own last illness.

Less than a month after the death of their mother, Jack and Warren were sent to Wynyard, a boarding school in Watford, England. As if the two brothers weren't already miserable, this turned out to be a wretched place, an ugly building of pale yellow brick with poor facilities. Wynyard had only one classroom and one dormitory and no library, laboratory, or athletic fields. The sickroom doubled as a storage room, and the odor from the outdoor toilets often permeated the whole campus.

As bad as the school facility was, its master was even worse. Robert Capron, called "Oldie" by the boys, was a volatile and unbalanced man who seemed to positively take pleasure in caning the boys and abusing them verbally. He was much more keen on discipline than on learning, and his class sessions consisted of little more than rote memorization of dry facts and figures. In one case, Capron's disciplinary measures were so harsh that a student's family filed a suit against him, which was settled out of court in favor of the plaintiff. A few years after the Lewis brothers departed, Capron was certified as insane and the school was closed down.

Though both Warren and Jack wrote their father about the abject conditions at Wynyard, Albert Lewis seemed to dismiss this as the usual friction between a schoolmaster and the boys under his charge. In later years, Lewis accepted some of the blame for his father's never understanding just how unhappy he was at the school he called "Belsen," after the Nazi prison camp. In *Surprised by Joy,* Lewis explained that he may not have conveyed forcefully enough how much he hated life at Wynyard because he didn't want to be thought a coward or a crybaby. About Robert Capron himself, Lewis said it was easier to depict his tormentor to his father "as a buffoon than an ogre." (As discussed in the next chapter, Lewis would later depict that ogre, Robert Capron, as a buffoon, Uncle Andrew, in *The Magician's Nephew.*)

Part of the regimen at Wynyard was mandatory attendance at a nearby church with high Anglican services. Lewis later said he first came to serious faith at that time in his life. Unfortunately, this newfound belief did not provide him with assurance or comfort, but created self-condemnation. He fell into an internalized legalism, such that his private prayers never seemed good enough. He felt his lips were saying the right things, but his mind and heart were not in the words. In those boyhood years at Wynyard, he was trapped in a religion of guilt, not grace. More and more, he came to associate Christianity with condemnation of others, as in the north of Ireland, or condemnation of oneself, for not living up to God's standards. When he was in his early teens, Lewis decided to put away childish things, including his Christian faith.

After leaving Wynyard School, Lewis spent a term at Campbell College, near his home in Belfast, but dropped out after only one term due to illness. The next year, he traveled to Cherbourg House, a private boarding school in the town of Malvern in Worcestershire. Jack was much happier at Cherbourg, largely, it seems, because of the matron there, who acted as a surrogate mother for the boys. In *Surprised by Joy,* Lewis described her with the same affection he had expressed in his earlier depiction of his childhood nurse. He concluded his portrait of the matron at Cherbourg House with a revelatory summation: "We all loved her; I, the orphan, especially."

One of the striking features of the Narnia stories is the absence of parents. In every case, Lewis creates some device— a father in India, a sick mother, children removed from home because of air raids over London—so that the children are required to face grave dangers and resolve difficulties on their own. Of course, this is a narrative device one often finds in children's stories, for an excursion into enchanted worlds accompanied by one's parents would be a much tamer sort of adventure. But the persistent motif of missing parents in the chronicles seems more than just a storyteller's convention; it appears to be linked to Lewis's loss of his mother and his sense of isolation during his years in English schools. In *Surprised by Joy,* he notes that after his mother's death, everything that makes a house a home failed him, and he and Warren became "two frightened urchins huddled for warmth in a bleak world."

After Cherbourg House, Lewis moved on to Malvern College, a preparatory school in the same town. He was intensely unhappy there, loathing the required sports and the clique of boys who formed a self-appointed elite. After Lewis spent two years of misery there, his father eventually arranged to have him study with a private tutor in Great Bookham, Surrey. Living with this outspokenly atheistic tutor, William Kirkpatrick, Lewis found his unbelief reinforced by his reading in the natural sciences and the social sciences. From the former, he gained a sense that life on earth is just a random occurrence in a vast, empty universe, that all of human history is no more than a teardrop in the vast ocean of eternity. From the latter, he concluded that all the world's religions, including Christianity, could best be explained not as claims to truth but as expressions of psychological needs and cultural values.

Throughout his middle teens, Lewis found his intellect and his imagination increasingly at odds. His rational side told him that life on earth is essentially without meaning or purpose. But his imagination continued to soar into worlds unknown and possibilities unseen. During his adolescence, Lewis lived daily with what he described later as a painful paradox: "Nearly all that I loved I believed to be imaginary; nearly all that I believed to be real I thought grim and meaningless."

"A Great Literary Experience"

Despite his intellectual skepticism during those years, Lewis never lost his sense of wonder or his love of enchantment. If his reason had truly reigned, he would have quickly dismissed anything written by George MacDonald, the nineteenth-century Scottish preacher, poet, and fantasy writer. But when Lewis, at age seventeen, discovered MacDonald's *Phantastes,* it was an emotional and spiritual watershed. Reading the story for the first time in the spring of 1916, Lewis wrote enthusiastically to a friend that he'd had a "great literary experience" that week, and the book became one of his lifelong favorites. Over a decade later, Lewis wrote that nothing gave him a sense of "spiritual healing, of being washed" as much as reading George MacDonald.

Phantastes (1858) is an episodic, dreamlike book, rich with spiritual overtones. It tells the story of a young man named Anodos, literally "one who has lost his way," whose mother died when he was a child. Reading a fairy tale one night, Anodos wishes he could travel to an enchanted wood, and his wish comes true the next day. He finds that he has come into fuller harmony with the world of nature, understanding the conversation of trees and animals and discovering in himself a "capacity for simple happiness" that he had never felt before. Anodos meets a beautiful young woman, pale and cold like marble (rather like the White Witch in *The Lion, the Witch and the Wardrobe*), who tries to lure him to his destruction. He escapes her clutches and undergoes a series of further adventures, including an encounter with an evil ash tree and a battle with a giant wolf. In the end, Anodos undergoes a symbolic death in the world of Fairy and returns to this world with "a power of calm endurance" he had not known before.

MacDonald's story is a singular and peculiar tale, sometimes disjointed in plot and uneven in style. Its evil tree spirits make it seem like a children's story, while its temptresses give it an air of adolescent romance. But there are spiritual meditations throughout the story that are clearly the work of a mature philosophic mind. Whatever its oddities, *Phantastes* was for Lewis a great balm to the soul, not only in his youth but throughout his lifetime. In his twenties, Lewis said that reading MacDonald served for him almost like devotional meditation. He also explained what he found so compelling in the Scotsman's fantasies: "The quality which enchanted me in his imaginative works turned out to be a quality of the real universe, the divine, magical, terrifying, and ecstatic reality in which we all live."

The Spires of Oxford and the Trenches of France

After finishing his preparatory work with William Kirkpatrick, Lewis entered University College, Oxford, in April 1917. But he had barely arrived in the famous university town when his education was interrupted by World War I and a two-year stint in the British army. In June 1917, he joined a cadet battalion billeted in Oxford, where his roommate was Edward F. C. "Paddy" Moore. The two soon became friends, and Paddy introduced Jack to his mother, Mrs. Janie King Moore, then forty-five, and his eleven-year-old sister Maureen.

Before they were shipped off to France, Jack and Paddy pledged to each other that if one of them did not return from the fighting, the other would do his best to look after the parent left behind. Jack arrived at the front lines on his nineteenth birthday, November 29, 1917. In February of the following year, he developed a case of trench fever and spent a month in a French hospital. In April, he was wounded in three places by an English shell that fell short. He had to be evacuated first to a mobile hospital in France, then back to England.

In that same spring of 1918, Paddy was reported missing in action and confirmed dead by the end of the summer. During his convalescence, Jack was never able to convince his father Albert, still in Belfast, to visit him in an English hospital. Yet Mrs. Moore came often; the bereaved mother and the abandoned son turned to each other for strength and consolation. During that time, Lewis in effect exchanged parents, gaining a new mother and all but losing a father. When Jack returned to Oxford in 1919 to resume his studies, he finished out his last

year of required residence, then
moved in with Maureen and Mrs.
Moore. Before long, he
began introducing her as
his mother, and the two
stayed together for over
thirty years, until her
death in 1951.

While he was conva-
lescing, Jack put together a collection of poems he'd written about love
and war that also expressed his personal
philosophy at that time. Titled *Spirits in
Bondage,* the book was published by William
Heinemann in March 1919 under the pseudo-
nym Clive Hamilton, in honor of his deceased mother. The
poems in this volume are often bleak, cursing an absent god and
suggesting that human love and art are all that keep life from
being utterly futile. In one poem, "Satan Speaks," the young
Lewis compares Nature to an evil spirit, one who causes humans
and other creatures to breed and to seek survival but offers them
no larger purpose for existence. In the closing stanza of the
poem, Nature, personified as Satan, concludes,

> *I am the wolf that follows the sun*
> *And I will catch him ere day is done.*

This is an allusion to Fenris the Wolf in Norse mythology, a great
beast who symbolizes destruction and chaos. In some versions,
Fenris swallows the sun on Ragnarok, the day of doom, killing
even Odin himself, chieftain of the gods, bringing about the end

of the world and the twilight of the gods. In this poem, the wolf image suggests that ultimately all human aspirations and dreams will come to nothing as the forces of Nature eventually bring an end to our world, its sun, and the human race itself. This wolf reappears as Fenris Ulf, the head of the White Witch's secret police in *The Lion, the Witch and the Wardrobe*. He is slain by Peter the High King in the climactic battle at the end of the book. Within the Christian worldview that informs the Narnia chronicles, it is not death and chaos, but Aslan and his followers who ultimately prevail. (In the original English editions, this character's name is Maugrim. The name Fenris appears in all American editions until 1994, when the publisher, HarperCollins, decided to revert to the original English texts.)

When Lewis returned to University College after the war, he resumed his studies in the humanities. That autumn, he met Owen Barfield, and the two became lifelong friends. Barfield was born in November 1898, the same month and year as Lewis, and like Lewis, he was educated in private schools and served in World War I before beginning his studies at Oxford. Lewis and Barfield had the kind of friendship that thrives on incessant debate, honing each other's minds like steel sharpens steel. It was Barfield who first critiqued Lewis's materialistic point of view, arguing that if human thoughts are merely an evolutionary survival tool, they should not be trusted as accurate reflections of reality. For Barfield, the mind is to reality as the eye is to light; it perceives what is actually out there, however partial or distorted those perceptions may be. Lewis would eventually dedicate his magisterial *The Allegory of Love* (1936) to Barfield, "wisest and best of my unofficial teachers."

Lewis completed his Oxford studies with great distinction, earning first-class degrees in classics (1920), ancient philosophy (1922), and English literature (1923). In the academic year 1924–25, Lewis accepted a one-year appointment as a lecturer and tutor in philosophy, a position that afforded him the opportunity for broad and careful reading in philosophy, from ancient to modern. In 1925, he was elected a Fellow at Magdalen College, Oxford, a position in English language and literature.

Having lived with a "divided mind" in his teens and early twenties, Lewis's intellect, imagination, and spiritual intuitions began to coalesce in his mid- to late twenties. For a brief period in his late teens, he took a keen interest in the occult and the paranormal, thinking that perhaps an empirical approach to spirituality might be more fruitful than the Christianity he had learned as a child. But gradually his interest waned as he found the new "scientific" approach was just as inconclusive as the older religious ones and that it required just as much faith. He was also disappointed in the Spiritualists he met at Oxford, who seemed to him egocentric, obscurantist, and essentially unspiritual. When Mrs. Moore's brother, John Askins, suffered a complete psychic collapse after dabbling for many years in occultism, Lewis decided to avoid what he called "Magic" and stick to "the beaten track, the approved road."

The Journey Back to Faith

As he studied formal philosophy in his twenties, Lewis moved away from his adolescent atheism and became interested in various forms of idealism. Whether it was described as the Absolute by a philosopher such as F. H. Bradley or as the Life Force by Henri Bergson, the idealists stressed an impersonal but godlike power behind the mask of the material world. Lewis was willing to grant that the material world might be an illusion, that deeper realities might lie in the world of the spirit. But more and more, he wanted to know if the Absolute, or Life Force, had a mind or not. If it was not Mind, then it had no more spiritual significance than gravity or solar radiation. But it if was Mind, then he wondered if it had a will, if it was on a higher moral plane than human minds. Gradually, in his late twenties, Lewis began to feel that the sophisticated idealism of the philosophers was leading him back to the simple faith of his childhood. He sensed, perhaps more by intuition than intellect, that he was grappling with something—or Someone—concrete and personal. As he wrote to Owen Barfield in a tone of humorous panic, "Terrible things are happening to me. The 'Spirit' or 'Real I' is showing an alarming tendency to become much more personal and is taking the offensive, and behaving just like God. You'd better come on Monday at the latest or I may have entered a monastery."

In the summer of 1929, at age thirty, Lewis converted to theism, believing in a personal God but not quite sure how to define his newfound faith. He found himself increasingly attracted to Christian writers such as Samuel Johnson, George MacDonald, and G. K. Chesterton. He also found kindred spirits in the Christians he met at Oxford, especially J. R. R. Tolkien, then a professor of Anglo-Saxon language and literature at Exeter College. Tolkien began meeting with Lewis in the late 1920s to read and talk about his earliest Middle Earth stories, which were later published as *The Silmarillion* (1977), the prequel to his epic *Lord of the Rings* fantasy.

It was Tolkien, as well as another Christian friend, Hugo Dyson, who initiated a major change in Lewis's thinking in September 1931. In his Great Bookham days, Lewis had read Sir James Frazer's *The Golden Bough,* a massive study in comparative religion that traces the myth of the dying god in many times and cultures. As a teenager, Lewis concluded that there was nothing particularly unique about Christian narratives of a God who came to earth, died, and rose again. But Tolkien offered a different interpretation. He argued that all those dying god myths revealed a universal intuition that humans cannot save themselves, that they need redemption as a gift from some higher plane. Tolkien explained Christ's incarnation as the historical embodiment of the dying god myth, the universal story of one who gives himself for the sake of his people.

Tolkien's paradigm of Christ's incarnation as "true myth" was indeed good news for Lewis, providing him with the grand synthesis he had been seeking since he'd lost his faith in his early teens. He had been trapped between an imagination that gloried in nature, myth, and romance and an intellect that dismissed it all as a tale told by an idiot, signifying nothing. Besides giving weight and value to myth, this view affirmed the functions of imagination and the intellect as complementary, not competitive. Lewis would later call imagination "the organ of meaning" and intellect "the organ of truth." The first generates pictures, metaphors, and myths by which we understand the world. The second weighs, sifts, and analyzes, discerning which products of the imagination correspond most closely with reality. This view afforded Lewis a tremendous sense of recovery, a method for re-embracing what seemed to him his core identity since childhood—wonder, imagination, mythology, faith.

When Lewis experienced what he called a "re-conversion" to Christian faith in his early thirties, he decided that since his early teens, he had been moving in the wrong direction; his boyhood at English schools had been a kind of "fall" from childhood. If that were true, becoming a grown-up would be a further step in the wrong direction. Just as terms such as *nurse, child,* and *fairy tale* are nearly always positive in Lewis's books, including the chronicles, there is an opposite set of terms—*boy, school, grown-up,* and *practical*—that are usually negative, connoting dreary utility, false sophistication, a preoccupation with politics and profits over those things that truly nourish the spirit.

"The Towering Grandeur of Lewis" in His Middle Years

In bringing together intellect and imagination, a lifelong love of fantasy with a newfound confidence in faith, Lewis laid the foundations for one of the most remarkable writing careers of the twentieth century. In his teens, Lewis had warned a Christian friend about the danger of "intellectual stagnation" for those who embrace traditional religious beliefs, but this would not prove to be a problem for Lewis himself. In the first half of his life, his reputation as a writer rested on two slim volumes of poetry, both of which went out of print nearly as soon as they were issued. But in the second half of his life, he wrote more than forty books, including many acknowledged classics of their kind. As a literary scholar and critic, he is well known for *The Allegory of Love* (1936), *A Preface to Paradise Lost* (1942), *English Literature in the Sixteenth Century, Excluding Drama* (1954), and *The*

Discarded Image (published posthumously in 1964). His classic works of Christian apologetics and meditation include *The Problem of Pain* (1940), *The Screwtape Letters* (1942), *Miracles* (1947), and *Mere Christianity* (1952). Besides the chronicles, Lewis's fiction also includes the award-winning Space Trilogy—*Out of the Silent Planet* (1938), *Perelandra* (1943), and *That Hideous Strength* (1945)—as well as a highly regarded late novel, *Till We Have Faces* (1956).

Apart from his accomplishments as an author, Lewis was easily one of the most popular and respected lecturers in Oxford during the 1930s and 1940s. His lectures were often delivered to standing room–only crowds, even for Saturday morning sessions on obscure seventeenth-century poems that few students had ever read. Dame Helen Gardner called Lewis "by far the most impressive and exciting person in the faculty of English" at the Oxford of her student years. Another commentator, George Bailey, noted that it is "almost impossible to exaggerate Lewis's prestige in post-war Oxford." Bailey added that scholars in English at the time, some of them well-known names, were "only foothills in the shadow of the towering grandeur of Lewis."

While Lewis's intellectual life was extremely active during his middle years, his external life was more settled. In 1930, he moved with Mrs. Moore and her daughter Maureen into a house north of Oxford called the Kilns, named after the brick kilns on the property. Soon afterward, they hired a local country fellow, Fred Paxford, as a gardener and general handyman. Paxford was one of those endearing eccentrics who tried to plan for the worst so painstakingly that it seemed he never expected anything but the worst. He was devoted to Mrs. Moore and to

Lewis, whom he called "Mr. Jack." Lewis returned the favor by immortalizing Paxford as the lovable pessimist Puddleglum in *The Silver Chair.*

In 1932, Warren Lewis retired from the army and joined the others in the Oxford household. Both Lewis brothers felt a strong attachment to the Kilns and its surrounding property. Architecturally, it was a smaller version of their childhood home, Little Lea, an unusual design with two gables of equal height set off to one side. Perhaps this otherwise unremarkable house reminded them of the settled happiness of their childhood before their mother's death.

In the early 1930s, the two Lewis brothers began meeting with Tolkien and other like-minded friends to read and discuss their works in progress or just to revel in one another's company. This informal group became something of a literary circle, which Lewis humorously dubbed the Inklings, taking the name from a defunct undergraduate club. Meeting on Thursday evenings in Lewis's rooms at Magdalen College, they read their compositions aloud and offered one another frank, if friendly critiques. Soon, Tuesday morning meetings in a local pub were added. In the 1930s and 1940s, an Inklings meeting might include, on any given week, the Lewis brothers and Tolkien, as well as the novelist Charles Williams, the physician Humphrey Havard, the attorney Owen Barfield, and a number of other friends who lived in and around Oxford.

Lewis's public visibility continued to grow throughout the 1940s. During World War II, he was invited to lecture on Christianity to members of the Royal Air Force, and he spent most weekends during the war years traveling to bases all over Great Britain. He also gave four series of radio talks on the BBC, which were later collected as *Mere Christianity* (1952). As Lewis's books became more and more popular, he created a charitable fund in which he deposited two-thirds of his book royalties, even though his salary as an Oxford don was by no means extravagant.

Apart from the increased attention that Lewis began to receive as the Narnia chronicles were published, the early 1950s brought other changes into his life as well. In January 1951, Mrs. Moore died, after several years of physical and mental decline. In 1954, he accepted a position that had been created just for him, professor of medieval and Renaissance studies at Magdalene College, Cambridge University. Though he retained this prestigious post until he retired in 1963, Lewis took the train home to the Kilns most weekends to be with his brother and his Oxford friends.

Late Love and Loss

In September 1952, Lewis met Joy Davidman for the first time. An atheist and a communist in her youth, Joy had become a Christian, partly through reading Lewis's books, and she began writing to him in 1950. Her letters to Lewis stood out from mountains of other fan letters as unusually witty and lively, so she was established as one of his more notable pen friends by the time they met face to face.

When Lewis first met Joy, she was Joy Davidman Gresham, the wife of American novelist Bill Gresham and mother of two sons, David and Douglas. The marriage was under severe strain, and when a breakup came, Joy and her two sons moved to England permanently in 1953. Joy was divorced from

 Gresham in 1954, and gradually, her friendship with Lewis deepened into something more than friendship. When the English Office refused to extend Joy's visa, Lewis agreed to marry her in a civil ceremony in 1956 in order to give her English citizenship. Some of those closest to Lewis objected to this, but he felt, perhaps naively, that a civil ceremony was a mere formality that would not affect their actual relationship.

In October 1956, Joy was diagnosed with bone cancer. The news seems to have changed her relationship with Lewis; within a few months, it was clear their companionship had ripened into love. The two were married in an Anglican ceremony in her hospital room in March 1957. By then, Joy's cancer was in an advanced stage; she was confined to bed in a great deal of pain. When she was released from the hospital in April, it was assumed she had only weeks to live.

Mr. and Mrs. Lewis had a temporary reprieve in her last years, as she became strong enough to walk and to accompany Jack on a visit to Ireland in the summer of 1958. By the autumn of 1959, however, the bone cancer had returned. Despite her deteriorating condition, the Lewises traveled to Greece with friends in the spring of 1960. Joy Davidman Lewis died in July 1960 at forty-five years of age—nearly the same age at which Lewis's mother had died.

Jack's own health was not good in the years following Joy's death. He suffered from heart and kidney disease and began receiving blood transfusions in 1961. He had a heart attack in July 1963 and went into a coma. After receiving last rites, he surprised everyone by waking up from his coma and asking for a cup of tea. Though he was comfortable and cheerful, Lewis never fully recovered from this condition. He died quietly on November 22, 1963.

Lewis assumed his books would go out of print not long after his death, and he worried about how well his brother Warren could support himself on his army pension. Lewis was always weak with numbers but strong on humility. He would have been astonished to learn that most of his forty books would still be in print a generation after his death, his popular books perennial best-sellers and his scholarly books required texts in graduate schools and seminaries. Nor could he have guessed that his literary estate, like that of his friend Tolkien, would later be valued in the millions of dollars. Though both men were distinguished scholars, the two might have had a good laugh if they had known it was their "holiday fiction" that ensured for both of them a lasting literary legacy.

CHAPTER TWO

The Genesis of Narnia

At the age of fifty, C. S. Lewis felt his powers as a writer were on the wane. In January 1949, he wrote a friend, "I feel my zeal for writing, and whatever talent I originally possessed, to be decreasing; nor (I believe) do I please my readers as I used to." Explaining that Mrs. Moore's ill health and increasingly uncertain temper were creating difficulties, Lewis concluded that he would try to find contentment whether or not he were able to produce any more books: "If it shall please God that I write more books, blessed be He. If it shall not please Him, again, blessed be He. Perhaps it will be the most wholesome thing for my soul that I lose both fame and skill lest I were to fall into that evil disease, vainglory."

Actually, Lewis's expressive powers were not at all in decline. It was his talent as a prophet that proved deficient. His skill as a writer was never more evident than in the books he wrote in his fifties, including his classic exposition of Christian faith, *Mere Christianity* (1952), his erudite but readable volume for *The Oxford History of English Literature* (1954), and his lively

27

memoir *Surprised by Joy* (1955). And Lewis's fame would climb to new heights with the publication of *The Lion, the Witch and the Wardrobe* in 1950, followed by the other Narnia chronicles in the next six years: *Prince Caspian* (1951), *The Voyage of the "Dawn Treader"* (1952), *The Silver Chair* (1953), *The Horse and His Boy* (1954), *The Magician's Nephew* (1955), and *The Last Battle* (1956). The culminating book in what his friend Roger Lancelyn Green dubbed the "Narnia Chronicles" won the prestigious Carnegie Medal for the best work of children's fiction published in that year.

It should be noted that the chronicles were originally published in a different order than that found in the editions currently in print. Most Lewis scholars agree that first-time readers of the Narnia stories should read them in the order they came out, so as to enjoy more fully Lewis's imagined world as it unfolded in his mind. However, Lewis once wrote to a little boy, agreeing that the books might be best read according to "Narnian chronological time," which would be *The Magician's Nephew, The Lion, the Witch and the Wardrobe, The Horse and His Boy, Prince Caspian, The Voyage of the "Dawn Treader," The Silver Chair,* and *The Last Battle.* Lewis suggested the same order to his secretary, Walter Hooper, so that is the way the chronicles have been numbered in the HarperCollins editions since 1994. This chapter will discuss the seven books in the order in which they were composed.

Despite his concern about his waning powers, Lewis seemed to produce the chronicles with comparative ease. He dashed off the first five in less than three years between the summer of 1948 and the spring of 1951. He began *The Last Battle* in the autumn of 1952 and finished it the following spring. *The*

Magician's Nephew, the most autobiographical story in the series, gave Lewis more trouble. He took up this tale soon after completing *The Lion, the Witch and the Wardrobe,* but didn't finish it until all the other chronicles were completed in the spring of 1954.

The Lion, the Witch and the Wardrobe

Lewis himself recognized that the process of creating the chronicles went back much further than his sitting down to write *The Lion, the Witch and the Wardrobe.* In an essay called "It All Began with a Picture," he explained that "the *Lion* all began with a picture of a Faun carrying an umbrella and parcels in a snowy wood. This picture had been in my mind since I was about sixteen. Then one day, when I was about forty, I said to myself: 'Let's try to make a story about it.'"

Actually, when he was "about forty," Lewis got only one paragraph into his first Narnia story. At the beginning of World War II in September 1939, Lewis's household at the Kilns accepted children who were evacuated from London during the air raids. Lewis pronounced the refugees "delightful" and said they gave him a newfound appreciation for children. Their presence seemed to give Lewis the idea for a story, so he began on an odd scrap of paper:

"This book is about four children whose names were Ann, Martin, Rose and Peter. But it is most about Peter who was the youngest. They all had to go away from London suddenly because of Air Raids, and because Father, who was in the Army, had gone off to the War and Mother was doing some kind of war work. They were sent to stay with a kind of relation of Mother's who was a very old Professor who lived all by himself in the country."

That seems to be as far as Lewis got with his Narnia tales until he casually remarked to an American scholar, Chad Walsh, in the summer of 1948 that he was hoping to complete a children's book he had begun "in the tradition of E. Nesbit." Edith Nesbit (1828–1924) was one of the few children's writers whom Lewis himself had enjoyed as a child. She wrote three books about the adventures of the Bastable children in *The Story of the Treasure Seekers* (1899), *The Wouldbegoods* (1901), and *The New Treasure Seekers* (1904), stories in which brothers and sisters enter into their adventures together, much like the Pevensie children in the chronicles. Nesbit also wrote three fantasy stories, *Five Children and It* (1902), *The Phoenix and the Carpet* (1904), and *The Story of the Amulet* (1906), all of which contain small plot elements that reappear in Narnia.

There has been no shortage of speculation about why a world-famous Christian apologist and literary critic nearing fifty would take up the humble genre of children's fiction. A. N. Wilson, the Lewis biographer who plays up a controversial angle whenever he can, argues that Lewis was bested in a philosophical debate with the meticulously logical philosopher Elizabeth Anscombe in February 1948. Wilson concludes that Lewis came away feeling that he could better express his Christian worldview in imaginative fiction than in intellectual forums. But philosopher Richard L. Purtill has countered this thesis, showing that the famous debate was not the one-sided pummeling Wilson makes it out to be and that Anscombe herself didn't think Lewis was particularly traumatized by the encounter.

Another of Lewis's biographers, Roger Lancelyn Green, has given himself some of the credit for the chronicles, noting that his own foray into children's fiction, a manuscript called "The Wood That Time Forgot," stimulated Lewis's interest and enthusiasm. That may well be, but Lewis seems to have already had the story in his mind, and he already had the example of other friends writing children's fiction, including Owen Barfield, who published *The Silver Trumpet* in 1925, and J.R.R. Tolkien, whose *The Hobbit* came out in 1937. At weekly Inklings meetings throughout the 1930s and 1940s, Lewis was also hearing Tolkien read from his work in progress, the epic fantasy that finally appeared as *The Lord of the Rings* in 1955.

Whatever served as the catalyst for the actual composition of the Narnia stories, it remains intriguing that Lewis, then in his sixties, should recall having the image in his mind of a faun with an umbrella since he was "about sixteen." At about that age—seventeen, to be precise—Lewis first discovered George MacDonald's *Phantastes*. As a child, Lewis had been no great reader of children's stories, except for those of Beatrix Potter and Edith Nesbit. So it was not perhaps until his reading of *Phantastes* that Lewis first felt the emotional depth and spiritual richness that a fantasy story could contain.

That faun with an umbrella that Lewis had carried in his imagination for over thirty years became, of course, Mr. Tumnus in *The Lion, the Witch and the Wardrobe*. Tumnus is the first character we meet in Narnia, the one who invites Lucy to his cozy little cave, where he lights a lamp, offers her a spot of tea, originally planning to lull her to sleep and then betray her to the White Witch. Though Tumnus is too decent a faun to go through with the scheme, his behavior, and the terrible woman he fears, call to mind the Maid of the Alders in *Phantastes*. She too is a white lady who is both beautiful and cold; she too invites the protagonist, Anodos, to her cave, where she lights a lamp and lulls him to sleep. And she too plans to betray her innocent guest. Unlike Tumnus, she has no second thoughts about her scheme: Anodos escapes with his life only through the good offices of a passing knight.

Of course, noting that MacDonald's Maid of the Alders looks somewhat like the White Witch and acts somewhat like Tumnus is not the same as saying *Phantastes* is the key creative source for *The Lion, the Witch and the Wardrobe*. Lewis's literary imagination was more like a river fed by many streams than like a machine in which Gear A set in motion Wheel B.

Lewis generally disliked source criticism, the interpretive approach that assumes major characters and images in a story can usually be traced to something in an author's life or reading habits. For one thing, he found that such guesses, however plausible, were often wide of the mark. He noted, for example, how many reviewers interpreted Tolkien's *Lord of the Rings* as an allegorical warning about the dangers of the atomic bomb. But Tolkien had already composed his epic fantasy before ever having heard of that new and fearful weapon. Apart from their wrong guesses, Lewis also warned that source critics may expend so much ingenuity in "getting behind the text" that they lose sight of the text itself.

Though Lewis distrusted source criticism, he did not try to argue that creative ideas appear out of nowhere. In fact, he believed the very idea of *creativity* takes on different connotations for those who believe in an ultimate Source. In a letter to his friend and fellow author Sister Penelope, Lewis wrote:

"Creation" as applied to human authorship seems to me
an entirely misleading term. . . . We re-arrange elements He has provided. There is not a vestige of real
creativity *de novo* in us. Try to imagine a new primary
color, a third sex, a fourth dimension, or even a monster which does not consist of bits of existing animals
stuck together! Nothing happens. . . . Writing a book is
much less like creation than it is like planting a garden
or begetting a child; in all three cases we are only entering as *one* cause into a causal stream which works, so to
speak, its own way. I would not wish it to be otherwise.

In discussing sources for the chronicles, Lewis was generally straightforward and obliging, especially in letters to children. For example, referring to *The Lion, the Witch and the
Wardrobe,* he wrote that "Everything began with images: a faun
carrying an umbrella, a queen on a sledge, a magnificent lion."
In a letter to a little girl named Anne, Lewis explained he had
made Aslan a lion because Christ is called the Lion of Judah and
because the lion is considered the king of beasts. He added that
he had been dreaming of lions about the time he started the first
of his Narnia stories. Reinforcing Lewis's choice perhaps was
the lion who acts as protector in Edmund Spenser's *Faerie
Queene,* Book I, as well as the Charles Williams novel that Lewis
found so impressive, *The Place of the Lion* (1931).

Lewis's image of a queen on a sledge, of course, became the
White Witch who casts a spell on Narnia so that it is "always win-
ter and never Christmas." Besides the Maid of the Alders in Mac-
Donald, this witch reminds us also of Hans Christian Andersen's
Snow Queen, another pale, cruel beauty who holds a little boy
captive. In *The Lion, the Witch and the Wardrobe,* she is identified as

a daughter of Lilith, the first wife of Adam who, according to Jewish folklore, became a mistress of the devil and a menace to children. To a reader who was wondering which witch is which, Lewis identified his White Witch with the sorceress Circe in the *Odyssey,* who turned Odysseus's sailors into swine. To help sort out all these possible sources, Lewis added that his villain is "the same Archetype we find in so many fairy tales. No good asking where any author got *that.* We are all born knowing the Witch, aren't we?"

With so many majestic lions and magical ladies to choose from, it is clear we need to take seriously Lewis's idea of an archetype. Borrowing from the psychologist Carl Jung (1875–1961), Lewis believed that a "fairy tale liberates Archetypes which dwell in the collective unconscious." That is, all readers (or those with a similar cultural heritage) share deeply embedded images and meanings that are evoked in myths, legends, stories, and even dreams. For Lewis, a well-constructed story draws upon these universal images and meanings. Much of the thematic richness of the chronicles derives from Lewis's skill in drawing on mythic patterns—the god who dies and comes back to life, the voyage to the end of the earth, the flight to freedom, the rescue of captives from the underworld, the beginning and the end of all created things.

The chronicles reward many rereadings because of this archetypal layer beneath the adventure layer. What Lewis said about space travel stories provides his justification for fantasy writing in general: "No merely physical strangeness or merely spatial distance will realize the idea of otherness which is what we are always trying to grasp in a story about voyaging through space: you must go into another dimension. To construct plausible and moving 'other worlds' you must draw on the only real 'other world' we know, that of the spirit."

In *The Lion, the Witch and the Wardrobe,* the gateway into the otherworld of Narnia is a wardrobe. In fantasy stories, the portal itself doesn't seem to matter much. In *Alice's*

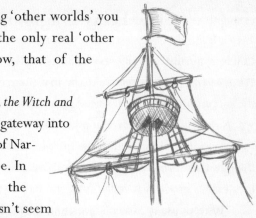

Adventures in Wonderland, it is a rabbit hole. In *Phantastes,* it is an oak desk. Lewis's choice of a wardrobe for the first of his Narnia stories seems most likely derived from the large wardrobe in Little Lea, into which the children used to climb to hear stories from "Jacks." That wardrobe does not have a looking glass on the front, like the one in the story. But the mirror never serves any narrative function in *The Lion, the Witch and the Wardrobe.* Perhaps Lewis added that detail to remind us of Lewis Carroll's *Through the Looking Glass,* another doorway into wonderland.

Of course, one needs to take care in one's choice of portals. When Lewis sent Owen Barfield a draft of *The Lion, the Witch and the Wardrobe,* Barfield's wife Maud was concerned lest children read the story and accidentally lock themselves inside a wardrobe. Lewis took this cautionary note to heart and ended up adding *five* warnings to *The Lion, the Witch and the Wardrobe* about not closing the door and locking oneself in. After the story was published, a little boy in Oxford took a hatchet and chopped a hole in the back of a family wardrobe, hoping to find his own way into Narnia.

The Lefay Fragment

Lewis originally had only one Narnia story in mind. *The Lion, the Witch and the Wardrobe* seemed to be that story, since it connected the pictures he'd had in his head into a satisfying narrative. But when Roger Lancelyn Green asked him how a lamppost came to be standing all by itself in the middle of the Narnian woods, the question seemed to require a creative answer. It was another mysterious image that called for a story to go with it.

In response to Green's question, Lewis decided to write a story about Narnia's origins, featuring Professor Kirke as a boy named Digory, along with his friend Polly. This book turned out to be his greatest creative challenge of the series, and Lewis did not finish his original sequel until all the other chronicles had been written. This was *The Magician's Nephew,* originally published sixth in the series (in 1955), but now numbered as the first of the chronicles, since it describes the very beginnings of Narnia.

Lewis's original beginning for *The Magician's Nephew* was never used and is now called *the Lefay fragment,* after a character named Mrs. Lefay. This version begins on a strongly satirical note: "Once there was a boy called Digory who lived with his Aunt because his father and mother were both dead. His Aunt, whose name was Gertrude, was not at all a nice person. Years ago she had been a schoolmistress and bullied the girls. Then she became the headmistress and bullied the mistresses. Then she became an inspector and bullied the headmistresses. Then she went into Parliament and became a Minister of something and bullied everybody."

After this sardonic opening, we soon learn that Digory was born with the gift of being able to communicate with trees and animals. As soon as his officious aunt is out of the house, he goes out to the grove of trees behind his house and rests in the branch-arms of a friendly old oak tree while chatting with the oak and a nearby birch. Soon a squirrel named Pattertwig joins them, offering Digory a nut and complaining that humans don't seem to do much "except killing animals or putting them in cages or cutting down trees." Then he hastens to add, "No offence, Digory: we all know you're different."

Soon Digory notices a girl in the backyard next door, trying to build something. Her name is Polly, and when she asks who Digory's been talking to, he keeps his gift a secret and says he's discovered a tame squirrel in the woods. Polly wonders if they could catch it and says she read in a book how to trap squirrels. Though she can only hear the chattering of a squirrel and the rustling of leaves, Digory hears Pattertwig taking offense at this conversation, while the oak complains, "That's what comes of chattering with humans. I knew she'd been wanting to eat him or skin him or shut him up."

Polly's building project is a raft, which she wants to launch in a nearby stream that flows into an underground culvert. She hopes to explore what she conceives to be "the bowels of the earth." Digory agrees to join the expedition but notices that her raft needs another crosspiece to hold the logs together. Polly suggests sawing a limb off the old oak tree for that purpose. Digory hesitates at first, but Polly badgers him about not being able to use a saw, about being afraid of what the grown-ups might say, and about being a big baby, until finally he climbs up a wall and begins sawing off a branch. The oak tree says nothing, but one of its limbs gives Digory a good swat in the face. As a thunderstorm descends, he insists on finishing the job before going inside to get out of the rain.

The next day, Digory returns to the wood to apologize to the old oak but discovers to his horror that he can no longer talk to the trees or understand the language of animals and birds. He returns to his house, feeling wretched and ashamed, and there he meets his godmother, Mrs. Lefay, "the shortest and fattest woman he had ever seen." She wears a black dress covered with gold dust and carries a black bag holding her rabbit Coiny, out for his afternoon ride. Mrs. Lefay seems to know all about Digory's terrible secret, telling him he looks like Adam five minutes after he'd been driven out of the Garden of Eden. Seeming to have some sort of mission in mind for Digory, she gives him a card with her address on it and offers complicated directions for finding a furniture shop that sells birds and pictures.

"Then you must go into the shop and you will see"; the manuscript breaks off in the middle of Mrs. Lefay's instructions, literally halting in midsentence. What was it Digory was supposed to see? That was as far as Lewis got with his first opening of what would later become the "Genesis" of Narnia. One can only speculate on why Lewis broke off this version of the story, though the reasons may not be all that obscure. On hearing this narrative, Roger Lancelyn Green complained that Mrs. Lefay seemed too much like a burlesque fairy godmother, and Lewis was inclined to agree. Also, in this first draft, Lewis broke some of his own rules about this sort of storytelling. In his preface to *That Hideous Strength,* Lewis explained that fantasy stories should be anchored in the real world; their characters begin in ordinary circumstances until they are swept into the world of Faerie. But in this version, Digory is born enchanted, able to converse with trees and animals, with no explanation given.

For whatever reason, Lewis abandoned this fragment altogether and later started afresh. Of course, that is not to say the creative effort here was wasted. As we already know, Digory and Polly would reappear in *The Magician's Nephew,* where Digory's Adamic fall would be less ecological and more theological. In that same book, Mrs. Lefay never appears, but she is mentioned, not as a good sort of fairy godmother but as the bad sort who dabbles in sorcery and ends up in prison. Pattertwig makes his appearance as one of the Talking Beasts in *Prince Caspian,* and Aunt Gertrude turns up as the Head of Experiment House in *The Silver Chair.* (In that version, she gets her comeuppance— being elected to Parliament—not at the beginning of the story but at the end.)

All in all, one can see Lewis's reasons for abandoning the Lefay fragment. Yet it contains many promising elements and is enjoyable to read in it own right. For someone with Lewis's gift for fantasy writing, even an artistic "failure" can be more intriguing than the "successes" of other writers with lesser talent.

Prince Caspian

In discussing the Narnia chronicles as a series, Lewis explained that he started with *The Lion, the Witch and the Wardrobe,* and after that "Aslan pulled the six other Narnian stories after Him." Having set aside his first attempt at a Narnia creation story, Lewis took up *Prince Caspian* next, completing it by December 1949. His original idea for this story was to show what a magical summoning is like from the point of view of the one called. In most stories, the magic words are spoken or the lamp is rubbed and a genie or other helper appears. But Lewis wondered what it would be like to tell the story from the other perspective. How would it feel from the other side? So he begins *Prince Caspian* with the Pevensie children sitting in a train station in England one year after the adventures described in *The Lion, the Witch and the Wardrobe*. Suddenly they are all four pulled irresistibly out of our world and back to Narnia. Later in the story, they will learn someone in that world had blown Susan's magical horn and had thus drawn them across time and space. Lewis originally called this story "Drawn into Narnia," but the publishers found that too hard to pronounce. He then tried "A Horn in Narnia," but they didn't accept that title either. The story would eventually take the full title of *Prince Caspian: The Return to Narnia*.

Of course, the idea of describing a magical summons from the reverse point of view is only the starting point for a story, not a story in itself. This time, the Pevensie children enter Narnia in an era when Aslan has not been heard from in a long time, and they are called upon to help depose another evil and unlawful ruler, Miraz. When they first arrive, they don't even know where they are, because their royal castle, Cair Paravel, has become an overgrown ruin. Eventually, they come to realize that although only one year has gone by on earth, centuries have passed in Narnia, and their return to that world is as if King Arthur were to show up in our own era. Eventually, with Aslan's aid, the children help restore the rightful king, Caspian, to his throne and bring back the old Narnia of Talking Beasts and Walking Trees.

Lewis enjoyed stories about time travel, such as H. G. Wells's *The Time Machine* (1895), and he even tried his own hand at the creating one. After finishing *Out of the Silent Planet* (1938), Lewis began a sequel called "The Dark Tower," a story centering on a chronoscope, a device for viewing our world in its past and future. Lewis abandoned the story after sixty-four pages, seeming to lose the thread of the plot in abstract speculations about the nature of time. But he returned to the idea in *That Hideous Strength* (1945), where the wizard Merlin reawakens in the modern era after lying for many centuries in a "parachronic state," in a time frame parallel to ours.

Long before the current discussion of multiple universes, Lewis was fascinated by the idea of separate dimensions of existence, each with its own time and space. In *Miracles* (1947), he speculated that there might be "Other Natures" that have "no spatial or temporal relation to ours." He added, though, that these separate Natures might all be connected by "a single Supernatural source" who "might allow *selected* events in one [Nature] to produce results in another." Of course, this is what happens every time someone from earth visits Narnia.

What is unique about Lewis's approach is that his time traveling does not occur in earth's time stream but in Narnia's. When Lucy first visits Narnia in *The Lion, the Witch and the Wardrobe,* she spends several hours with Mr. Tumnus, only to find later in the story that no time at all has elapsed on earth during her absence. Later on, the four Pevensie children grow to adulthood in Narnia, becoming kings and queens, but when they return to earth at the end of the story, they are the same age as when they began.

Lewis's creation of an "Other Nature" with its own time stream has both literary and spiritual implications. This literary device allows us to experience all of Narnia's history—thousands of years, from its creation to its apocalypse—within only one lifetime on earth. According to a time line for Narnia that Lewis once jotted down, his imagined world was created in about 1900 earth time and came to an end in 1949, the year the Pevensie children were in a train accident back in England. Thus, the entire sweep of Narnian history occurs in just about the time from Lewis's own birth until the time he started writing the chronicles.

For Lewis, though, the idea of differing time streams was not just a literary convenience but also a spiritual reality. He believed that time, like space, is created and that its Creator stands outside time and space. In this view, eternity is not an endless succession of years but a suspension of years, an everlasting now. Lewis believed that many apparent theological conundrums—free will versus determinism, God hearing millions of prayers all at one time—are caused by the mistaken premise that the Creator is inside of time instead of beyond it. As he explained in a letter, "Time is a defect of reality since by its very nature any temporal being loses each moment of its life to get to the next—the moments run through us as if we were sieves! God forbid that we should think God to be like that." After recommending Boethius's *Consolation of Philosophy* on the doctrine of the eternal now, Lewis ends with a familiar verse from the Bible: "With the Lord one day is as a thousand years, and a thousand years as one day."

The Voyage of the "Dawn Treader"

Lewis performed a bit of magic with time himself, completing one of his best-loved chronicles, *The Voyage of the "Dawn Treader,"* in less than three months, between December 1949 and February 1950. In his notes for this story, Lewis wrote that it could involve a magic picture that served as the portal between earth and Narnia. He envisioned it as a sea voyage, what he called a "very green and pearly story," with stops at various islands, as in the "*Odyssey* and St. Brendan." Lewis ended up not making much use of Homer's epic poem, unless one construes Eustace's turning into a dragon as similar to Odysseus's men being turned into beasts. But Lewis drew a great deal on the lesser-known odyssey, the medieval legend of St. Brendan and his voyage to the Land of Promise.

St. Brendan (484–577) is one of Ireland's most venerable saints and perhaps one of its most adventurous. The historical Brendan, called the Navigator, founded Christian centers of worship and learning not only in western Ireland but also in Wales, Scotland, Brittany, and probably the Faroe Islands, between England and Iceland. But a tenth-century Latin text, *Navigatio Sancti Brendani,* tells of a far more ambitious quest, all the way to an earthly paradise called the Land of Promise. Tales of Brendan's voyage were known throughout Europe in the Middle Ages, and for many centuries, he was better known than St. Patrick. Nearly all medieval and Renaissance maps of the Atlantic include a St. Brendan's Isle, although it is located everywhere from the Arctic to the Equator.

According to the *Navigatio Sancti Brendani* ("Voyage of Saint Brendan"), the great leader heard tales of a Land of Promise to the far west and proposed to seek it out for himself. He originally planned to take fourteen monks with him, but three latecomers were allowed to join the party. Setting out from the coast near Mount Brandon (the highest peak in Ireland, which is named after him), the explorers stop first at an island of rocky cliffs, where they find a great manor house, seemingly empty. After the host appears, one of the latecomers is caught stealing a silver bridle-bit, but he repents and is forgiven. When the voyagers set out again for the farther west, they come upon a pastoral island, which they name the Isle of Sheep, and one with trees full of birds, which they christen the Paradise of Birds. They disembark on a small islet in order to celebrate Easter, only to discover that they have inadvertently climbed onto the back of a whale, who turns out to be a friendly, frisky fellow whom they call Jasconius.

After being driven by a storm and sailing in circles for a while, the voyagers are chased by a malevolent whale and pass an Isle of Sleep shrouded in mists. Then Brendan and his party reach a place of pellucid waters and see great crystal towers rising out of the sea and mountains spouting flames. They find a man clinging to a rock in the middle of the ocean, who turns out to be Judas, allowed a respite from hell on Sundays in the cooling waters of the turbulent sea. Just as the pilgrims are running out of provisions, a magnificent bird flies overhead and drops a bough on deck, laden with grapes the size of apples. Soon the boat comes to an island covered with grape trees that give off a delicious fragrance. There, the travelers rest and replenish their supplies.

Farther west, the voyagers meet a hermit, one hundred and forty years old, who is swathed in his own white hair and beard. He says his name is Paul and explains that he no longer eats at all but that in former times, his food was brought to him every day by an animal that walked on its hind legs. Paul prophesies that Brendan and the others will soon reach the island they are seeking.

Hermits in these old tales are wondrously reliable, and soon the voyagers reach a great island, seemingly the size of a continent, covered with fruit trees. This is the Land of Promise, the earthly paradise originally intended for Adam and Eve. Brendan and his crew explore for forty days, until they come to a great river too broad for fording. There, a handsome young man, seemingly an angel, tells them they were not meant to cross this river or stay in this land. The Land of Promise will not be inhabited until it is given to the Blessed at the end of time. And so Brendan sails back to Ireland, having been gone seven years. Despite all the hardships of his travels, he lives and thrives to the well-seasoned age of ninety-three.

Although many episodes in the *Navigatio* are clearly fanciful, there has always been a great deal of speculation about the historical basis for Brendan's legendary voyage. Geoffrey Ashe's *Land to the West: St. Brendan's Voyage to America* (1962) examines the historical underpinnings of the tale and finds them surprisingly plausible. Historically, the Irish did venture far out into the Atlantic in their curraghs, skin-covered boats, visiting the Faroe Islands (*Faroe* means "sheep" in Danish), and perhaps encountering crystal towers in the sea (icebergs) and flaming mountains (volcanic islands off Iceland). C. S. Lewis owned a copy of Ashe's book in the last years of his life. The photographs in the book must have been of particular interest to him, especially the picture of a reputed Celtic altar stone, found in New Hampshire, which looks exactly like the Stone Table as described in *The Lion, the Witch and the Wardrobe!*

Readers of *The Voyage of the "Dawn Treader"* can see many parallels between the two odysseys. As in Brendan's voyage, there are three latecomers—late indeed, as Edmund, Lucy, and Eustace join the *Dawn Treader* after it is already under way. One of the three latecomers, Eustace, is caught stealing. There is an island mostly inhabited by sheep, Felimath, and an island of sleep—or the worst part of sleep, nightmares. There is also an island with what seems a great empty house until its owner, the magician Coriakin, appears. And Ramandu, with his long white hair and beard, looks just like the hermit Paul. His island has a "dim, purple kind of smell," which reminds us of the island covered with grape trees. And here, birds prepare Aslan's Table every day, blending several incidents in the *Navigatio*—the Paradise of Birds, the supernatural feeding by a bird of brilliant plumage, and the animal who brings food to Paul every day.

Of course, Brendan's voyage to find the Land of Promise takes him west, whereas the *Dawn Treader's* mission, as its very name suggests, is to reach the utter East. But despite their opposite directions, both odysseys are what Geoffrey Ashe calls "Otherworld Quests." Though Caspian hopes to find out what happened to seven Narnian lords who set out to explore the Eastern Seas, his knight, the chivalrous mouse Reepicheep, pursues a more mystical quest: to find Aslan's country beyond the dawn. (Lewis's utter East may be an echo from a William Morris story, "The Land East of the Sun and West of the Moon.")

In summarizing the themes of his chronicles to a girl named Anne, Lewis wrote that *The Voyage of the "Dawn Treader"* was about "the spiritual life (especially in Reepicheep)." In another letter, this time to a group of children, Lewis explained that the valiant mouse is not an allegorical figure but that "anyone in our world who devotes his whole life to seeking Heaven will be *like* Reepicheep."

In many ways, Reepicheep, with his elegant sword and flowery speech, seems more a comic figure than an exemplar of "the spiritual life." But he has been haunted all his days by words he first heard in his cradle from his nurse, a wood nymph:

> *Where sky and water meet,*
> *Where the waves grow sweet,*
> *Doubt not, Reepicheep,*
> *To find all you seek,*
> *There is the utter East.*

Reepicheep says he has been under the spell of this rhyme all his life and he intends to seek out the utter East and, possibly, to reach Aslan's country. Obviously, the rhyme evokes in the noble mouse a kind of Sweet Desire, like the piercing pleasure the young Lewis felt on reading Longfellow's lines about Balder. If the young Lewis heard the call of "Northernness," Reepicheep might be said to be under the spell of "Easternness."

At the end of the odyssey, the *Dawn Treader* nearly runs aground near the World's End. But Reepicheep casts away his sword and sails over the edge in a coracle, or "skin boat." He vanishes from the sight of the others, but the narrator tells us he believes Reepicheep really did make it safely to Aslan's country (a guess that is confirmed in *The Last Battle*). Ultimately, as critic Evan Gibson has noted, Reepicheep is the true Dawn Treader of this odyssey.

The Horse and His Boy

After finishing his story about a voyage to the utter East in the spring of 1950, Lewis focused his next chronicle, *The Horse and His Boy,* on characters whose goal is to reach "Narnia and the North." Lewis wrote *The Horse and His Boy* in the summer of 1950, at the same time he was examining proof sheets for *The Lion, the Witch and the Wardrobe,* which would be published later that year. Rereading his first Narnia tale, Lewis may have recalled that he only offers a glimpse of the Pevensies as full-grown kings and queens of Narnia. The whole story of *The Horse and His Boy* takes place during the time described in the last chapter of *The Lion, the Witch and the Wardrobe,* when the Pevensie siblings have become Peter the Magnificent, Susan the Gentle, Edmund the Just, and Lucy the Valiant. This story is set mostly in Calormen, a great empire to the south of Narnia, separated from it by the mountain kingdom of Archenland and the Great Desert.

The Horse and His Boy is a double escape story, about a runaway peasant boy named Shasta and a runaway princess named Aravis. Shasta learns to ride a Narnian Talking Horse, Bree, in order to escape being sold as a slave to a red-bearded Calormene warlord. Aravis also rides a Narnian horse, Hwin, seeking to escape an arranged marriage to an old man whom she despises. After being chased toward one another by lions, the four fugitives join forces, heading for freedom in the lands to the north.

When they come to the great city of Tashbaan, Shasta is mistaken for Prince Corin of Archenland, and he briefly meets King Edmund and Queen Susan before escaping back to the streets. Later, he spends a lonely night among the ancient tombs outside the city. There, on the edge of the desert, Shasta is comforted by a large cat who, in some sort of dream, seems to turn into a lion in order to frighten away jackals who have ventured dangerously close. Meanwhile, Aravis overhears a plot by Prince Rabadash of Calormen to invade Archenland and Narnia. Shasta on Bree and Aravis on Hwin ride hard through the desert, chased by yet another lion, until they reach the safety of the Hermit of the Southern March. Just as he is about to lose hope, Shasta meets Aslan in the dead of night and learns the true nature of his adventures. It was Aslan who seemed to be two lions chasing the riders together. It was also he who took the form of a cat to comfort Shasta at the tombs, frightened away the jackals, and chased the two exhausted horses to the safety of the hermitage.

Shasta reaches the king of Archenland just in time to warn of the surprise attack, and the Archenlanders and their Narnian allies defeat the Calormene invaders. Even in defeat, Prince Rabadash will not be appeased, and Aslan casts a spell on him, turning him into an ass, declaring that he can only resume human form if he stays within ten miles of the center of Tashbaan. Shasta learns that he is actually Cor, a lost prince of Archenland. Eventually, he becomes its king, with Aravis joining him as queen.

Lewis explained that he found the name Aslan, which is Turkish for "lion," in a copy of *The Thousand and One Nights* (which Lewis referred to as the *Arabian Nights*). More specifically, he said he saw the word in a footnote of Edward William Lane's classic translation, *The Arabian Nights' Entertainments, or The Thousand and One Nights* (1840). The Aslan of *Arabian Nights* is a noble young man whose father is falsely accused of stealing from the caliph. Aslan undergoes a series of adventures in order to save his father from the hangman and restore his family's good name. There is nothing unusual or supernatural about this young man in the story; Lewis seems to have just remembered the name and its meaning.

In an unpublished letter, Lewis mentioned that his overall depiction of Calormen was also influenced by *Arabian Nights.* He explained that he never enjoyed this collection of tales, either as a child or an adult. This may seem surprising to those familiar with Aladdin and his lamp or Sinbad the sailor. But in reading an unabridged, scholarly translation such as Lane's, one finds few stories suitable for children. These folktales, which originated in Cairo and Baghdad between the eighth and tenth centuries, tell of cruel and bloodthirsty caliphs, abducted and tortured women, mistreated slaves, and starving street people. And all these characters, of high station and low, are plagued by evil jinn and devilish, shape-shifting Efreets.

The Horse and His Boy offers a greatly toned-down version of the violent, demon-haunted world of *Arabian Nights.* Many of the details of the story seem derived from *The Thousand and One Nights* as translated by Edward William Lane, the most distinguished Middle Eastern scholar of his generation. In *Arabian Nights,* we see narrow, walled streets, as in Tashbaan, with wealthy nobles and their viziers carried on litters, forcing their way through the crowds. The city streets abound in cats, some of whom turn out to be Efreets in disguise. These evil jinn may take the form of a lion or any other animal, which recalls the

Calormene belief that Aslan and the Talking Beasts of Narnia are actually demons. In several stories, slaves, or even wives, are whipped for real or imagined offenses. In one story, a man is punished by being transformed into a donkey.

Apart from the text itself, Lane's scholarly notes to *Arabian Nights,* which run to over three hundred pages, seem also to have contributed details to *The Horse and His Boy.* As already mentioned, Lewis said he found the name Aslan in Lane's notes. These voluminous notes also describe the extensive burial grounds outside an Arabian city in terms similar to those Lewis uses to describe the tombs where Shasta spends the night. The notes also mention that it was against religious law in medieval Arabia to color one's hair black but that one might hide the gray by dyeing one's hair with henna, which was called "gazelle's blood." This note helps explain an odd detail in *The Horse and His Boy*—the Calormene warrior Anradin, whose crimson beard is noted several times in the story.

In many ways, the exotic scenes of Calormen re-present the *Arabian Nights,* transposed into the world of the chronicles. Since Lewis admitted that he didn't enjoy Lane's book, it makes sense that the main story line of *The Horse and His Boy* is not about living in Calormen but about trying to escape that world to Narnia and the north.

The Silver Chair

Having completed *The Voyage of the "Dawn Treader"* by the spring of 1950 and *The Horse and His Boy* by the end of the summer, Lewis started his next chronicle, *The Silver Chair,* in the autumn, finishing it by March 1951. Once he has shown his readers the uncharted oceans east of Narnia and the mountains and deserts to the south, his next chronicle carries them off to badlands in the north. In this tale, Eustace Scrubb and Jill Pole are commissioned by Aslan to rescue Caspian's son Rilian, who is being held captive. Lewis originally called the story "The Wild Waste Lands" and then considered "Night Under Narnia" or even "Gnomes Under Narnia."

As those last two titles suggest, Lewis planned this story so that his protagonists would have to accomplish their mission by going underground—literally. *The Silver Chair* is another kind of archetypal story, the journey to the underworld. This is a familiar motif in many world mythologies, including Egyptian, Greek, Roman, Norse, and Celtic. In many such myths, the purpose of such a journey is to bring back a captive from regions below. Thus, Hercules, in one of his mightiest deeds, finds Alcestis and frees her from the abode of the dead. In another myth, Orpheus tries to rescue his wife Eurydice, who has been bitten by a snake and has descended into Hades. Orpheus fails because, disobeying instructions, he looks back to see her face before she has emerged into the upper world. The early Christians treated the descent into the underworld as another of the true myths, universal stories that point to genuine spiritual truths. The apostle Paul wrote that Christ descended into the lower parts of the earth, leading "captivity captive" when he ascended again. Peter wrote that Christ preached to the spirits in prison in the time between his death and resurrection.

The Queen of Underland is another archetypal figure, a lamia—part woman, part serpent. She is what might be called a "hissing cousin" to the White Witch in *The Lion, the Witch and the Wardrobe.* Glimfeather the Owl tells Eustace and Jill that she is of the "same crew" as the sorceress who bound Narnia in ice and snow for a hundred years. And later on, a dwarf explains, "Those Northern Witches always mean the same thing, but in every age they have a different plan for get-

ting it." Like her cousin, this queen is associated with Lilith, who turns into a serpent in George MacDonald's version of the story. In Spenser's *Faerie Queene,* an enchantress called Error turns into a serpent and tries to wind her body around the Red Cross Knight in the same way the Queen of Underland tries to wrap up Prince Rilian. At the narrative level, the Queen of Underland is another usurper, one who hopes to rule by guile or might, not by right. At the mythic level, she is an evil spirit, the adversary of all that is good.

Standing against this formidable foe are only two children, Eustace and Jill, and their friend, Puddleglum the Marshwiggle. This froggy fellow, who always expects the worst, is the only character in the chronicles who is based on someone Lewis actually knew at the time when he was writing the Narnia stories. Puddleglum is Fred Paxford the gardener, carried off to Narnia and transformed into a marsh-wiggle. Like Paxford, he is full of comic eccentricities, but he is ultimately someone of solid character and sound judgment who can be counted on in a crisis. Though Lewis didn't like to talk about his books much, he confessed to Walter Hooper that he considered Puddleglum, along with Reepicheep, one of his most successful creations in all the Narnia stories.

The Last Battle

Once he had finished *The Silver Chair,* Lewis made a fresh go at the story of Narnia's beginnings in the autumn of 1951, writing about three-quarters of a new version of the story about Professor Kirke as a boy. But once again, he wasn't sure about the overall structure of the story, and he set it aside for another two years. He ended up writing *The Last Battle* first, finishing it in March 1953, then going back to revise *The Magician's Nephew* in the winter of 1953–1954.

The last of the Narnia stories presents some of the most depressing scenes in all the chronicles, followed by some of the most glorious. The opening words of the book, "In the last days of Narnia," make it clear from the outset that this will be an account of that world's apocalypse. Shift the Ape presents a simple-minded donkey, covered in a lion's skin, as Aslan returned after a long absence. This new, angry lion is not at all like the Aslan of past ages. He allows living trees to be cut down, Narnians to be enslaved, and Calormenes to enter as an occupying army. When the rightful Narnian ruler, King Tirian, protests all this as a horrible sham, he is taken prisoner by Calormene soldiers. He calls out in desperation to the friends of Narnia from another world, and before long Eustace and Jill arrive, as they had on their mission to rescue Prince Rilian in *The Silver Chair.* This time, though, things are beyond putting right, and the two children will join in watching the destruction of the old Narnia.

The main story line of *The Last Battle* is obviously drawn from Bible passages about the end times, especially Matthew, chapter 24, and the book of Revelation. In a letter to a child,

Lewis identified Shift the Ape as a kind of Narnian Antichrist. The narrative includes many other biblical details, such as believers who are led astray, great battles, and, finally, the very dissolution of the natural world.

With his typical creative synthesis, though, Lewis also draws on one of Aesop's fables to tell the story of Narnia's final days. Aesop tells of a donkey who finds a lion's skin and spreads it over his back. At first, everyone who meets the lion is afraid and treats him with great respect. But when he tries to roar, out comes a donkey's bray and everyone sees through his disguise. The fox tells the foolish ass that when you are pretending to be something you are not, you had best keep your mouth shut. In *The Last Battle,* Shift the Ape is much more clever than Aesop's donkey, and he does all the talking.

The closing chapters of *The Last Battle* offer a seamless blend of Greek philosophy, Christian eschatology, and Norse mythology. Narnia comes to an end, but the scene is not mere devastation and calamity. It is all orchestrated by Aslan. This is a kinder, gentler apocalypse than one finds in either the book of Revelation or in Norse myths of the twilight of the gods. The stars fall from the sky, not as a sign of utter chaos but because Aslan has "called them home." Great beasts devour the landscape, and the world ends in a rising sea and a blast of cold, as in the Norse Ragnarok. But this is only the end of time-bound Narnia. As Digory explains, quoting Plato, that created world was only a copy or image of the eternal Narnia, as our earth is an image of the new heaven and new earth mentioned in the book of Revelation. Night may have fallen on the created Narnia, but here there will be no twilight, only eternal morning.

The Magician's Nephew

As mentioned earlier, Lewis struggled more with creative blocks in writing *The Magician's Nephew* than he did with all the other chronicles combined. He began writing a story in the summer of 1949 to explain the origins of Narnia, soon after finishing *The Lion, the Witch and the Wardrobe*. But his Lefay material came to an abrupt halt after twenty-six handwritten pages. Two years later, he tried again, getting about three-quarters of the way through a whole new draft. Then he went on another creative detour, some chapters based on the medieval poem "Piers Plowman" that have not survived. After another two years had passed and all the other chronicles were written, Lewis finally went back and completed *The Magician's Nephew* early in 1954. Roughly speaking, Lewis wrote all the other chronicles in a six-year span from 1948 to 1953. But it took him six years, writing on and off between 1949 and 1954, to complete *The Magician's Nephew*. Lewis seemed unable to write his Narnian "Genesis" until he had completed its apocalypse, an odd illustration of the old paradox of how the first shall be last.

Perhaps Lewis struggled with this material because it drew so heavily on his personal experience, especially the untimely death of his mother and his traumatic years in English boarding schools. The very first page of *The Magician's Nephew* offers a number of details that recall Lewis's own childhood. In the opening paragraph, we learn that the story takes place "when your grandfather was a child." Lewis was a grandfatherly fifty-seven when this story was published. Its central character, Digory Kirke, has a mother who is terminally ill and an absent father. He also has what is called a "funny name" and spends a lot of time playing indoors because it is so rainy out—two familiar details in Lewis biographies. (Recall that when we first meet Digory in *The Lion, the Witch and the Wardrobe,* he is Professor Kirke, who, like his author, is a distinguished university professor willing to take in children who were sent away from London during the air raids of World War II.)

In addition to these general similarities, nearly every detail on the opening page of *The Magician's Nephew* echoes Lewis's early life. The narrator says his story is set in the same time Sherlock Holmes was solving crimes from his home in Baker Street and the Bastable children were hunting for treasures. He adds that it was also a time when schoolboys had to wear stiff Eton collars and the schools "were usually nastier than now." The Sherlock Holmes stories were at the height of their popularity when Lewis was young, and his friend Arthur Greeves used to come over and borrow copies of Conan Doyle's detective stories. Lewis himself was more partial to Edith Nesbit and her Bastable stories, which seem especially apt in this context because they are based on her own childhood memories. In his memoir *Surprised by Joy,* Lewis spends nearly a third of the book detailing how nasty the schools were in those days. He even complains about being "throttled by an Eton collar" on the day his father took him down to the Belfast quay to be sent over to school in England.

All his life, Lewis would be haunted by Robert Capron, the pitiless schoolmaster at Wynyard whom young Lewis had described to his father not as an ogre but as a buffoon. As a teenager, Lewis wrote that Capron would make a memorable villain in some as yet unpublished story. Almost forty years later, Lewis seems to have followed up his own suggestion. In the same year (1955) he published his memoir *Surprised by Joy,* portraying Capron as an ogre, Lewis also published *The Magician's Nephew,* portraying him as a buffoon.

Even in physical description, one is struck by the parallels between the brutal Robert Capron and the comical Andrew Ketterley. Uncle Andrew is described in *The Magician's Nephew* as "very tall and very thin," "with a sharp nose and extremely bright eyes." He also has "a great mop of tousled grey hair," which is referred to a half dozen times in the course of the story. Later in the book, we also learn that Uncle Andrew has turned sixty. In their family memoirs, Warren judged Capron to have been "about 60" when the Lewis brothers attended Wynyard, describing him as "above middle height" with "piercing eyes" that were nearly black, a small, deformed nose, and "plentiful grey hair." Capron was also remembered for his "Assyrian smile," suggesting not good will but guile, which reminds us of Uncle Andrew's malicious grin, variously described as a "cunning smile," a "cruel smile," and a "hateful smile."

Warren also explained in the *Lewis Papers* that Capron came from the southern county of Devonshire and that he took pride in his origins, ridiculing his pupils from the working class or from the northern counties. To the Lewis brothers, he had what they considered "a mincing, affected speech." He seemed to drop his *r*'s and not pronounce his vowels fully enough. Similarly, Andrew boasts several times of his "very old Dorsetshire family," referring to the county that borders on Devonshire. He pronounces "girl" as "gel," "damn" as "dem," and his disjointed speech is variously referred to as stammering, muttering, and babbling.

Though Uncle Andrew is an insidious character, he is also one of Lewis's most successful comic creations. Despite the many parallels, Andrew is ultimately someone who evokes not dread or loathing but laughter. In this instance, Lewis's parody seems to be a kind of pardon. By turning an ogre into a buffoon, he was able to transform fear and anger into pity and forgiveness, using his imagination to purge his heart.

Apart from personal sources, one can see again in *The Magician's Nephew* a creative synthesis of literary materials from Lewis's own favorites. The creation of Narnia, of course, draws heavily on the book of Genesis. Perhaps it is also colored by Tolkien's creation account in *The Silmarillion,* where the world is brought into being by a symphony of song. The "waxwork" images of all the kings and queens at Charn may owe something to a scene Lewis admired in *King Solomon's Mines,* in which adventurers discover a chamber full of petrified statues of chieftains. Queen Jadis is another of archetypal adversary, like her sister queens in *The Lion, the Witch and the Wardrobe* and *The Silver Chair.* (In fact, Lewis called Jadis a "white witch" in a letter, so this may in fact be the same character.) Jadis's brief visit to London and all the chaos she brings about certainly call to mind a similar scene in Edith Nesbit's *The Story of the Amulet,* where a Babylonian queen appears in London, with similar results.

That "in-between place," the Wood between the Worlds, seems to derive from a more remote source. Its name certainly owes something to William Morris's *The Wood at the End of the World* (1894), a work whose very title evoked in Lewis the painful longings of Sweet Desire. But the description of the wood itself, and its narrative function, seem influenced by Algernon Blackwood's *The Education of Uncle Paul* (1909).

Algernon Blackwood was a popular writer of mystical fantasies in the early twentieth century. In his teens, Lewis was a devoted reader of Blackwood, commenting favorably on books such as *John Silence: Physician Extraordinary* (1908), *Jimbo: A Fantasy* (1909), and *A Prisoner in Fairyland* (1913). Lewis was disappointed in Blackwood's later, more philosophical books, saying Blackwood was turning from a "good romancer into a bad mystic." The Blackwood story that Lewis wrote about most enthusiastically was the one with the dullest title, *The Education of Uncle Paul.* At the age of seventeen, Lewis wrote to his friend Arthur Greeves: "Oh, I have never read anything like it. . . . When you have got it out of your library and read how Nixie and Uncle Paul get into a dream together and went to a primaeval forest at dawn to 'see the winds awake' and how they went to the 'Crack between yesterday and tomorrow' you will agree with me."

In Blackwood's fantasy tale, Paul is a forty-five-year-old Englishman who is returning home after twenty years in America to live at a country estate with his widowed sister. Paul finds all of his sister's three children endearing, but especially the sprightly, blond-haired Nixie. One afternoon, as they are lying on the lawn, gazing at clouds together, Paul and Nixie seem to sink into the ground, re-emerging in a quiet place with trees in every direction and a slow-moving river. Nixie explains that they are in a dream together, in what Paul earlier called a "Beyond-World." Together, they watch the winds awaken, seeing curls and ribbons of angel hair all over the landscape that begin to swirl and grow incandescent with the rising sun. As Paul ponders this experience, he suddenly has a kind of epiphany about its meaning: "He realized vividly that *within* himself a region existed where all he desired might find fulfillment. . . . There existed this inner place within where he might visualize all he most wished for into a state of reality. The workshop of the creative imagination was its vestibule."

Later in the story, Nixie and her siblings take their Uncle Paul through the "Crack between Yesterday and Tomorrow" just as a clock is striking midnight. They say the crack gets smaller as you get older but that Paul can squeeze through because of his childlike spirit. Again they find themselves in the quiet place of trees and a smooth-flowing river. After several more visits, Paul decides that "'Between Yesterday and Tomorrow' is the children's counterpart of that timeless, deathless region where the spirit may always go when hunted by the world, fretted by the passion of unsatisfied yearnings, plagued by the remorseless tribes of sorrow and disaster." He concludes that anyone may find this place whose "Wanderlust of the spirit seeks ever for a resting-place in the great beyond that reaches up to God."

At the end of the tale, little Nixie dies of a sudden illness. Her Uncle Paul is overwhelmed with grief, remembering her, in an odd phrase to describe a little girl, as a "fine woman." But then he discovers that he can still meet her whenever he travels to that enchanted place, Between Yesterday and Tomorrow. The ending of the story is rather murky, anticipating perhaps Lewis's later concerns about Blackwood mixing good romance and bad mysticism. It suggests that somehow all the griefs and disappointments of this world can be overcome in a region of dreams, imagination, longing, and deathless spiritual bonds. Perhaps Lewis enjoyed Blackwood's book more for its imagery and enchanted atmosphere than for its philosophy.

The most striking similarity between Blackwood's Between Yesterday and Tomorrow and Lewis's "in-between place" in *The Magician's Nephew* is the quiet world with innumerable trees and still waters. Nixie explained to Uncle Paul that this is not a place where anything *happens;* it just *is.* Similarly, Digory explained about the Wood Between the Worlds, "It's not the sort of place where things happen. The trees go on growing, that's all." Lewis also remembered how Nixie and Paul had first entered this world by getting "into a dream together." In the chapter called "The Wood Between the Worlds," Lewis mentions more than a half dozen times that Digory and Polly feel they are in a dream or speak dreamily. In a more peculiar echo, Uncle Andrew, at the end of *The Magician's Nephew,* sums up Jadis as a "dem fine woman," recalling Uncle Paul's memory of his niece as a fine woman.

If Lewis did indeed remember the spell that Blackwood's enchanted wood had cast upon him in his teens, he may also have recalled the significance of the wood. Uncle Paul repeatedly interprets the wood as a place within himself, a vestibule of the creative imagination that could lead him to a "timeless, deathless region where the spirit may always go when hunted by the world." This sounds very much like what Lewis, in his discussion of fantasy literature, called the "Otherworld of the Spirit." Blackwood's mystical imagination called him to some "resting-place in the great beyond that reaches up to God." Lewis dreamt about lions, read the name Aslan, and imagined places where a dying mother might be made well. And then he created a world called Narnia.

CHAPTER THREE

The Spiritual Vision of the Narnia Chronicles

L ewis wrote an influential book called *Rehabilitations and Other Essays,* a collection of essays about authors he thought were undervalued or misunderstood. But perhaps the greatest rehabilitation project of his career was his ongoing commitment to rehabilitate people's conception of God. On one hand, he lampooned the notion of a capricious, hell-happy deity who is "extraordinarily kind and good to his [creatures] and would certainly torture most of them to death the moment he had the slightest pretext." On the other hand, he also satirized the giddy, vacuous theology in which God is pictured as a "grandfather in heaven—a senile benevolence" presiding over a universe in which "a good time was had by all." In Aslan, Lewis hoped to portray a God who is both awe-ful and good, inspiring equally a wholesome fear and a whole-hearted love.

Some readers assume Lewis had an explicit didactic purpose in mind when he created Narnia. They suppose he first decided to write something Christian for children, then chose the fantasy story as his vehicle, then studied theology and child psychology in order to create spiritual allegories for young readers. Lewis bluntly dismissed this view of his writing method as "pure moonshine," explaining that the world of Narnia began as a series of unconnected images—a faun, a pale queen, a magnificent lion. "At first there wasn't even anything Christian about them," he explained; "that element pushed itself in of its own accord."

As the story-making process matured, however, Lewis began to see the Christian possibilities in the narratives that were beginning to take shape. He remembered how in his own childhood, he had lacked any real sense of love or awe for God, feeling constrained by a sense of enforced reverence. He wondered if, by recasting Christian doctrines into "an imaginary world, stripping them of their stained-glass and Sunday school associations," he could "steal past those watchful dragons" of tedious sermons and obligatory worship. By enlisting the unfettered powers of imagination, Lewis hoped to recapture the original beauty and poignancy of the Gospel message. In this strategy, of course, Lewis succeeded admirably.

Despite their rich spiritual overtones, it does a great disservice to the chronicles to read them as allegories, as if all the major characters and incidents are merely disguised Bible stories. Lewis called his children's books "supposals," not symbols or allegories, explaining to one group of young inquirers, "You are mistaken when you think that everything in the books 'represents' something in this world. Things do that in *The Pilgrim's Progress* but I'm not writing in that way. I did not say to myself 'Let us represent Jesus as He really is in our world by a Lion in

Narnia': I said 'Let us *suppose* that there were a land like Narnia and that the Son of God, as He became a Man in our world, became a Lion there, and then imagine what would happen.'" What happens when God is portrayed as a lion in another world is not just classic children's fantasy. For many readers, the enduring appeal of the chronicles lies not so much in their literary art as in their probing theological insight.

Aslan as a Numinous Being

For those seeking a fuller understanding of the divine, Lewis often recommended Rudolf Otto's *The Idea of the Holy* (1923). Otto is the scholar who coined the term *numinous,* which he defined as a person's sense of overwhelming smallness and frailty in the face of "that which is supreme above all creatures." In studying the Bible and other sacred texts, Otto identified six common features of numinous experiences:

- Fear, awe, holy dread
- Fascination, attraction, yearning
- A sense of unspeakable magnitude and majesty
- Energy, urgency, intense dynamism
- Wonder, astonishment, stupefaction
- Mystery, Otherness, incomprehensibility

In *The Problem of Pain* (1940), Lewis used Otto's concept of the numinous to explain his own understanding of progressive revelation. Lewis argued that all cultures have left records of

numinous experiences, showing their awareness of a transcendent power and might behind the screen of the ordinary world. But the Old Testament offers the first clear recognition that the Almighty One is also the Holy One, that the numinous and the ethical emanate from the same Source. In the New Testament comes the final revelation, that the righteous God is also an atoning God, suffering with and for humanity in order to redeem it.

To illustrate what he meant by numinous experiences, Lewis gave examples from the Bible, such as Jacob's dream of a ladder to heaven (Gen. 28:17) and Ezekiel's vision of four-faced creatures and wheels full of eyes (Ezek. 1:18). Lewis also supplied examples of uncanny longing and dread from classics such as Aeschylus, Ovid, and Virgil. Amid these ancient and venerable sources, Lewis included a more homely illustration, a passage from Kenneth Graham's *The Wind in the Willows* (1908). In the scene where Rat and Mole approach the god Pan, Mole timidly asks his companion if he is afraid: "'Afraid?' murmured the Rat, his eyes shining with unutterable love. 'Afraid? Of Him? O, never, never. And yet—and yet—O Mole, I am afraid.'"

This folksy—or furry—example of the numinous sounds very much like a scene set in Narnia. Indeed, Lewis created many such episodes in the chronicles to evoke a sense of the numinous. In *The Lion, the Witch and the Wardrobe,* for example, when Mr. Beaver first explains to the Pevensie children about Aslan, Susan and Lucy wonder if meeting a lion might not be quite safe. "Who said anything about safe?" answers Mr. Beaver. "'Course he isn't safe. But he's good. And He's the King, I tell you." Later, when three of the Pevensie children, accompanied by Mr. and Mrs. Beaver, meet Aslan in person, the scene is highly reminiscent of the one Lewis so enjoyed from *Wind in the Willows.* They are quite shy and abashed in the presence of the great lion, and none of them wants to be the first to step forward. As the narrator explains, "People who have not been in Narnia sometimes think that a thing cannot be good and terrible at the same time. If the children had ever thought so, they were cured of it now."

Besides Rudolf Otto's *The Idea of the Holy,* Lewis also recommended Edwyn Bevan's *Symbolism and Belief* (1938), quoting it in his own books *The Problem of Pain* and *Miracles.* Bevan builds on Otto's discussion of the numinous, examining the metaphors and symbols people choose to describe the nature of the divine. Surveying world religions, Bevan notes that deity is most often associated with images of agelessness, height, and dazzling light. (Of this last trait, Bevan concludes poetically, "The numinous is luminous.")

Lewis made use of all these qualities in his portrayals of Aslan. The great lion is certainly ageless, described the same way on the day of Narnia's creation as he is on the day of its destruction thousands of Narnian years later. When the skeptical dwarf Trumpkin in *Prince Caspian* muses aloud that Aslan must be getting to be a "pretty elderly lion," Lucy comes close to losing her temper and Peter tells the dwarf solemnly that he is talking nonsense, that he should never speak of Aslan that way again.

Aslan is "the same yesterday, today, and forever," and he also lives in a place of unimaginable height. When Eustace and

Jill are called to Aslan's country in *The Silver Chair,* they find themselves at the edge of a high precipice. From where they stand, the tiny, white specks they see far below are actually great, billowy clouds in the sky above Narnia.

Aslan is also frequently portrayed as luminous. When Lucy hears him call her name in the dead of night in *Prince Caspian,* she has no trouble finding him, for he shines in the moonlight. When he meets Shasta in *The Horse and His Boy,* again at night, he appears with a "fiery brightness" and a "swirling glory." In *The Last Battle,* the Calormene nobleman Emeth compares Aslan to a flaming mountain and says he has "eyes like gold that is liquid in the furnace."

Aslan as Supremely Good

When Narnians say, "Aslan is not a tame lion," they refer both to his utter sovereignty and to his numinous qualities. He comes and goes as he pleases, seemingly absent from the world for centuries, then reappearing when least expected. And Aslan is certainly no one's pet. He does not appear simply to comfort and console; he sends his followers into battle, knowing some will not return. He also seeks not just outward submission on their part but transformation of their inner being. In *Mere Christianity,* Lewis called the idea of a Life Force a "Tame God" because it offers the consolations of religion with none of the cost. He contrasted this with the teachings of Christ, who says, "Be ye perfect," and vows to his followers that he will not rest, nor let them rest, until they are the kind of creatures in whom their

Father can be well pleased. Aslan has this same untamed quality, commanding obedience in his followers not for his sake but for theirs.

In *The Last Battle,* the phrase "Aslan is not a tame lion" is horribly misapplied by miscreants, as if he is subject to no law, no standard of right and wrong. Thus, Shift the Ape, in the name of a false Aslan, commands that Talking Beasts be enslaved and Living Trees cut down. Shift also claims that Aslan the All-Good and the demonic Tash are really images of the same Supreme Being. To these dreadful doctrines, King Tirian proclaims, "It is as if the sun rose one day and were a black sun."

This anguished cry in a world turned upside down echoes the thirteenth-century mystic Meister Eckhart. In proclaiming the absolute Otherness of God, Eckhart declared, "Calling God good is like calling the sun black. He is beyond any attributes we might name." It is not known whether Lewis knew this particular saying of Eckhart, but it is clear he emphatically disagreed with the idea. In Lewis's mind, we worship God not because he is the Supreme Being but because he is supremely good. Lewis argues, "The Divine 'goodness' differs from ours, but it is not sheerly different: it differs from ours not as black to white but as a perfect circle from a child's first attempt to draw a wheel." Lewis adds that even in their crude early attempts, the children understand what it is they are trying to imitate. Lewis would never allow that we worship the "mere power" of the divine, which he called "the most blackguardly of superstitions." To say "Aslan is not a tame lion" is to acknowledge his numinous qualities and his absolute sovereignty over Narnia. But what commands obedience to Aslan is right, not might.

Aslan's Many Forms of Presence

Lewis explained often that the Narnia chronicles are "supposals," an imaginative answer to the question of how God might manifest himself in other worlds. He was not trying to write Christian allegory, and thus it would have been heavy-handed to portray Aslan in explicitly Trinitarian terms, as Father, Son, and Lion Spirit. Yet the doctrine of the Trinity was central to Lewis's own spiritual vision—a sense of God as transcendent, beyond time and space, yet also incarnate, entering into our world, and also indwelling, a still, small voice within. Even in a supposal, we see these same dimensions of Godhead in the chronicles.

The idea of a Narnian Trinity is most strongly suggested in *The Horse and His Boy,* when the boy Shasta first meets the great lion face to face and asks who he is. Aslan simply answers "Myself" three times, first in a voice low and deep so as to shake the earth, then in voice clear and glad, then in a barely audible whisper that "seemed to come from all around you as if the leaves rustled with it." Lewis confirmed in a letter that Aslan's thrice-repeated answer was meant to suggest the Triune Deity.

Though less explicit elsewhere, a Christian understanding of the Trinity is assumed or hinted at in all the Narnia stories. In *The Lion, the Witch and the Wardrobe* we learn that Aslan is the son of the Emperor-Beyond-the-Sea, whom Lewis never attempts to portray directly in any of the chronicles. Though he was a great admirer of *Paradise Lost,* Lewis thought it was a mistake for Milton to try to depict God the Father enthroned in heaven. Book 3 of the epic poem describes God as a voice coming out of a luminous cloud, commanding legions of angels. The picture is meant to evoke mystery and majesty, but it comes off rather too much like blustery stage theatrics. Lewis thought it wiser to simply refer to the Emperor-Beyond-the-Sea, suggesting numinous majesty and transcendent inaccessibility without trying to show it. Aslan is the incarnate form of Deity—not just a spiritual presence but an actual embodiment. When the proud horse Bree presumes to dabble in Narnian theology in *The Horse and His Boy,* he explains that Aslan may be metaphorically considered strong as a lion or fierce as a lion, but it would be disrespectful to consider him an actual lion with paws and whiskers. Just then, Aslan appears, scaring the wits and the shallow philosophy out of Bree and commanding the cowering steed to draw near: "Do not dare not to dare. Touch me. Smell me. Here are my paws, here is my tail, these are my whiskers. I am a true Beast." As so often happens, Narnian incidents, while not allegorical, have biblical parallels. It is hard to read this scene without thinking of Christ's words to "doubting" Thomas, inviting him to touch the wounds in his hands and his side.

Besides the Emperor-Beyond-the-Sea and Aslan, there is no explicit third person of the Narnian trinity. But as Walter Hooper has pointed out, the biblical words for *spirit* (Hebrew *ruach,* Greek *pneuma*) can both be translated "breath" as well, and Aslan expresses his spirit in breathing upon his creatures. It is his breath that transforms chosen animals on the day of Narnia's creation into Talking Beasts. And it is breath that turns the White Witch's victims from stone statues back into living creatures. This scene calls to mind a passage in *Mere Christianity* where Lewis says that humans are born with *bios,* physical life, which decays and dies, but not *zoe,* spiritual life, which is eternal. He says the world is like a great sculptor's studio and we are all statues waiting to come to life.

Aslan's father and his spirit appear in the chronicles mainly by allusion or suggestion. It is Aslan himself, of course, who is by far the main expression of God's nature as imaginatively portrayed in Narnia. But Aslan is not a tame lion, and sometimes he is not any kind of lion. In *The Horse and His Boy,* he is the cat who comforts and protects Shasta among the tombs outside Tashbaan. In *The Voyage of the "Dawn Treader,"* he first appears as an albatross who leads the ship out of dread darkness. Later, he is the Lamb who welcomes the voyagers as they near Aslan's country (reminding readers of another name for Christ, the Lamb of God).

Although the portrayal of Aslan as a lion, king of beasts, is a brilliant master metaphor for Lewis's imaginative supposal, he seemed to feel as the chronicles developed that one metaphor alone was not enough. In *Symbolism and Belief,* Edwyn Bevan observed that the faith of the Hebrews as recorded in the Old Testament is one of the least anthropomorphic of ancient world religions. While most other religions usually visualized incarnated gods in human form, the Lord God of the Israelites appears as a burning bush, a cloud of pillar and fire, a voice out of whirlwind, and a still, small voice.

Lewis adopted a similar strategy in the chronicles, depicting Aslan in several forms and in many different roles in order to express the myriad dimensions of God's nature. In the closing pages of the final Narnia story, *The Last Battle,* Aslan explains that the Shadowlands have passed away, and he no longer appears to those around him as a lion. Instead, the faithful experience something "great and beautiful" beyond describing. In the new and everlasting Narnia, words fail and all metaphors fall short of the glory.

Aslan as Creator

In *The Magician's Nephew,* Narnia begins as a dark void, until a voice begins to sing the most beautiful music ever heard. The deep, resonant sound is joined by "cold, tingling, silvery voices," and suddenly the night sky above is ablaze with stars. The First Voice then swells to a crescendo and up rises a new sun, seeming to "laugh for joy." The newborn light reveals mountains and valleys and a great river, but the whole terrain is bare and barren of life. The glow of that first morning also reveals the great lion, and his new song of "gentle, rippling music" calls forth grass and heather and trees. Then the earth begins to bubble like boiling water, and out of the bursting mounds come every variety of beast, joined by showers of birds emerging from the trees.

From this ebullient menagerie, Aslan selects certain animals, always in twos, male and female, touching his nose to theirs, calling them apart from others of their kind. These he breathes upon and, with a flash like fire, he finally speaks: "Narnia, Narnia, Narnia, awake. Be walking trees. Be talking beasts. Be divine waters." Those who have been called respond, "Hail, Aslan. We hear and obey. We are awake. We love. We think. We speak. We know."

This creation story echoes the book of Genesis, of course. But it is broader than the biblical account. In Lewis's imagined world, humans do not arise from the earth; rather, they come to Narnia from our own earth. In one of his earlier fantasies, *Perelandra* (1943), Lewis described "the old definition" of humans as "*animal rationale*—an animal, yet also a reasonable soul." A reasonable soul is one with a moral sense and a rational sense, with free will and the power of speech. In Genesis, this *imago Dei,* "image of God," is bestowed only upon men and women. In the chronicles, Lewis combines his biblical worldview with his love of myths and fairy tales. Aslan breathes his likeness into animals, creating Talking Beasts. He also creates fauns and satyrs and even bestows "reasonable souls" upon trees and waters, creating dryads (tree nymphs) and naiads (water sprites).

Aslan as Co-Sufferer

In the Narnian Genesis, the fall takes place even before creation. In a moment of rashness and spite, Digory Kirke rings a bell on the dead world of Charn, thus awakening the witch Jadis and eventually bringing her to the unspoiled world of Narnia. This mistake will be paid for by Digory, by the Narnians, and, most of all, by Aslan. By allowing his free creatures to move between worlds, Aslan permits evil to enter what might otherwise have become a new Eden.

In the last book he wrote before his death, *Letters to Malcolm: Chiefly on Prayer* (1964), Lewis speculated about what it must have cost an all-good Creator to breathe life into beings who could choose between good and evil. Lewis wondered if there might have been "an anguish, an alienation, a crucifixion in the creative act," God bringing into being that which is finite, temporal, fallible, fall-able. Lewis asked if God, in withdrawing his sovereignty in order to make room for the free will of creatures made in his likeness, might be seen as a "Tragic Creator" before becoming a "Tragic Redeemer."

In *The Magician's Nephew*, Lewis gives an imaginative embodiment to his speculation about a God who shares the affliction of his children. Unlike the biblical Adam, Digory Kirke is given a chance to undo some of the harm caused by his wrong choice. Aslan calls upon Digory to travel to a distant garden in the west and return with a silver apple to protect the newly created land from the witch's evil designs. Digory's mother back on earth is dying, and he can't help but blurt out a question to the great lion, asking if anything can be done for her. When he despondently raises his eyes to meet Aslan's, he receives one of the greatest surprises of his life: the lion has great tears in his eyes, as if he were sadder about Digory's mother than the boy himself. "My son, my son," sighs Aslan, "grief is great. Only you and I know that in this land yet. Let us be good to one another."

Despite their shared sorrow, Aslan explains that he must attend first to the safety of Narnia. He sends Digory off on a winged horse to fetch the apple that will protect that world for many years. Digory must undergo another temptation, as Jadis tries to convince him to keep the apple for himself and use it to heal his mother. But he does as he was told and returns to Aslan with the apple. In the end, Narnia is kept safe and Digory's mother is miraculously healed. Though Lewis's own mother died when he was nine years old, he suggests in his fiction that God will someday wipe away all tears and that, more than we know, he understands those tears.

Aslan as Redeemer

When Digory journeys west to find the magic apple, he learns not only about obedience but also about acting for the sake of others, not for oneself. The tree he seeks is enclosed by a high wall, and on that wall is inscribed in letters of silver:

Come in by the gold gates or not at all,
Take of my fruit for others or forbear.
For those who steal or those who climb my wall
Shall find their heart's desire and find despair.

Despite the witch's serpentine arguments that he should keep the apple for himself, Digory does as he has been commanded, earning that resounding "Well done!" from Aslan and guaranteeing that the newly created land of Narnia will enjoy many long years of peace before it is again troubled by evil. In placing the protection of Narnia above his own heart's desire to heal his dying mother, Digory shows that he understands well the words written on the golden gates.

The words on the garden entry offer a poetic expression of what Lewis called the "Principle of Vicariousness." In *Miracles,* he explains that even in the natural world, "everything is indebted to everything else, sacrificed to everything else, dependent on everything else," whether flowers and bees or predators and prey. Lewis goes on to explain that this natural ecology finds an even higher expression in sacred history, first in the chosen people, who are "chosen not for their own sake . . . but for the sake of the unchosen," and finally in the "Sinless Man [who] suffers for the sinful."

In a letter to his friend Arthur Greeves, Lewis interpreted Vicariousness, the idea of inescapable interdependence, not just as something found in nature or history but as one of the most pervasive principles of human life: "It [is] the rule of the universe that others can do for us what we cannot do for ourselves and one can paddle every canoe *except* one's own. That is why Christ's suffering *for us* is not a mere theological dodge but the supreme case of the law that governs the whole world: and when they mocked him by saying, 'He saved others, himself he cannot save,' they were really uttering, little as they knew, the ultimate law of the spiritual world."

Although Digory's willingness to act for others will keep Narnia safe for many a long year, it does not fully make up for his great mistake on Charn. Aslan explains, "Evil will come of that evil, but it is still a long way off. And I will see to it that the worst falls upon myself." That prophecy comes true in *The Lion, the Witch and the Wardrobe* with Aslan's own sacrifice for the sake of Edmund. After siding with the White Witch and betraying his siblings, Edmund learns, in the school of suffering, how foolish he has been and how cruel she truly is. But Edmund's sincere repentance, even his bravery in battle and his forgiveness by the others, are not enough to balance the moral scales of Narnia. The Witch invokes the "Deep Magic," a law engraved on the Stone Table: any traitor, like Edmund, must forfeit his life as her lawful prey. Aslan offers his own life for Edmund's, enduring a night of lonely sadness like Christ in the garden of Gethsemane and then a day of humiliation and death like the Passion. But beyond the Deep Magic the Witch knows about, the condemnation of law, is the Deeper Magic, Aslan's fulfilling of the law and his triumph over death.

Aslan's sacrificial death and his return to life are so artfully por-trayed in *The Lion, the Witch and the Wardrobe* that many readers get swept

up in the story and don't stop to ponder its biblical overtones. Pauline Baynes, the famous illustrator for the original edition of the chronicles, confessed she was in tears while drawing this scene for the book, but its parallels with Christ's suffering didn't occur to her at the time.

Other readers may err in the opposite direction, analyzing these chapters in *The Lion, the Witch and the Wardrobe* as a direct expression of Lewis's theology. Some have complained that this scene offers an inadequate view of atonement because Aslan offers his life not for a fallen race but for only one person, Edmund, whose sins have already been paid for in our own world. Others wonder why Aslan would ever strike a bargain with the White Witch, as God would certainly have no such dealings with the devil.

Lewis sometimes responded to such criticisms by offering reminders to scholars that are like the ones he sent to school-children. To one seminarian, Lewis explained, "You must not confuse my romances with my theses. In the latter I state and argue a creed. In the former much is merely supposed for the sake of the stories." Instead of trying to extract a particular theology from the climactic scenes of *The Lion, the Witch and the Wardrobe,* it may be wiser to simply acknowledge them as the most moving portrayal of vicariousness, "the Sinless who suffers for the sinful," to be found anywhere in Lewis's books.

Lewis's depiction of Aslan's sacrifice may well have been influenced by the book *Windows on Jerusalem: A Study in the Mystery of Redemption* (1941), written by his friend Sister Penelope, a biblical scholar and Anglican nun. When she sent him a copy of her book, Lewis replied that he found it a "real help," especially "the very important bit about Hebrew & Roman ideas of ransom." In her book, Sister Penelope explained that the Roman idea of ransom, like the modern one, involved paying a fee to obtain someone's freedom. The Hebrew word for ransom, by contrast, means "to act the part of a kinsman." For example, when Benjamin is (falsely) accused of stealing a silver cup from Pharaoh's household, his older brother Judah offers to become a slave himself until Benjamin's name can be cleared (Genesis, chapter 44). In the same way, Aslan acts the part of a kinsman in accepting the punishment intended for Edmund.

Lewis also complimented *Windows on Jerusalem* for its "really splendid account of how God can't help deceiving the devil." His reference is to Sister Penelope's contention that the devil, having "completely repudiated the Divine Likeness in himself, cannot recognize it in another." She goes on to explain that Christ on the cross opened himself to the Enemy's uttermost attack and that Satan thought that the Son, cut off from the Father, surely could not stand on his own. Enduring "the whole flood of the world's evil," the Son holds on and remains himself. As Sister Penelope concludes, "Before the Cross, the Enemy, who had thought to gain all, stands at the last weaponless and empty-handed."

In the climactic scene of *The Lion, the Witch and the Wardrobe,* the White Witch stands in much the same condition. The sacrifice described is not rightly called an atonement, because Aslan and Edmund were already reconciled, "at one," before the Witch claimed Edmund as hers according to the Deep Magic. The best summation of the Deeper Magic from before the dawn of time comes from Aslan himself. When Lucy asks, "Can anything be done to save Edmund?" the great lion answers, "All shall be done."

At the end of *The Voyage of the "Dawn Treader,"* Lucy is heart-broken at the idea of having to return to earth and leave Aslan behind. "'It isn't Narnia, you know,'" she sobs. "'It's *you*. We shan't meet *you* there. And how can we live, never meeting you?'" To Lucy's great comfort, Aslan tells her that she can meet him in her own world under another name: "This was the very reason you were brought to Narnia, that by knowing me here for a little, you may know me better there."

When a little girl named Hila wrote Lewis and asked about Aslan's other name, he replied that he wanted her to guess: "Has there ever been anyone in *this* world who (1) Arrived at the same time as Father Christmas. (2) Said he was the son of the Great Emperor. (3) Gave himself up for someone else's fault to be jeered at and killed by wicked people. (4) Came to life again. (5) Is sometimes spoken of as a Lamb. . . . Don't you really know His name in this world? Think it over and let me know your answer!"

Aslan's reply to Lucy, and Lewis's to Hila, remind us again of the author's strategy in writing the chronicles. The artist in him took simple delight in telling good stories and telling them well. But the spiritual mentor in him wanted to help readers steal past the "watchful dragons" of rote religion so that they could be dazzled anew by the treasures within.

Aslan as Comforter and Guide

Aslan's followers often find themselves on dangerous and demanding quests. But he also imparts the strength and guidance they need to fulfill those quests. Sometimes he does this by taking unexpected forms, such as the cat who comforts Shasta in *The Horse and His Boy* or the albatross in *The Voyage of the "Dawn Treader"* who whispers to Lucy, "Courage, dear heart." Often the guidance needed comes in the form of a vision or dream. In *Prince Caspian,* he calls Lucy's name in the middle of the night to help the group get back on the right path. (She knows she is awake, although the others tell her later that she must have been dreaming.) In *The Voyage of the "Dawn Treader,"* Eustace's "undragoning" occurs in the form of a dream, and its setting is not the island but rather somewhere in Aslan's country—a mountaintop with a well of living water. In *The Silver Chair,* the lion appears to Jill Pole in a dream, to help her understand the true meaning of the Signs she has started to forget. And in *The Last Battle,* King Tirian, tied to a tree, cries out for help to the friends of Narnia in other worlds, and he sees them back on earth in "a dream (if it was a dream) more vivid than any he had had in his life."

As is well known, dreams are often portrayed in the Bible as channels for divine communication—to Jacob, Joseph, Daniel, even to nonbelieving kings and pharaohs. Of course, this belief is much broader than Judeo-Christian tradition. There is very nearly a universal intuition that dreams convey truths hidden to the waking intellect. This can be found everywhere from classical myths and medieval allegories to modern therapies and self-help books. So Lewis was drawing on a very broad tradition in his use of revelatory dreams. But one wonders if he did not have some special fascination for the idea, for it appears in nearly every one of the chronicles. When asked once if he had a personal sense of spiritual realities, Lewis replied cryptically that he had never seen visions but that he had dreamed dreams. Then, characteristically, he added, "I don't think that matters a hoot," emphasizing the importance of simple obedience over the quest for esoteric experience. Yet in Narnia, dreams often provide valuable clues about the will of Aslan in the waking world.

Aslan as Judge

The whole last third of *The Last Battle* is an imaginative portrayal of an eternal otherworld where Aslan rules over all, where death is no more, and where the friends of Narnia from all generations may join together. On that eternal morning, they begin an adventure that will last for all time and beyond time. There too, in the new Narnia, every moral being's final destiny is revealed. But in Lewis's understanding, this moment of reckoning is not so much a Day of Judgment as a Day of Acknowledgment.

As all the talking creatures of that world come face to face with Aslan, they turn one way, to bliss and fellowship, or they turn another, into the shadow of the great lion and an unknown destiny. But the path they take, toward light or shadow, is not determined by Aslan's face as he looks at them. Rather, it is determined by *their* faces as they look at him. Some bear expressions of fear and hatred, and these cease to become "reasonable souls" at all, losing their powers of reason and speech. But others look upon him with reverence and love, even if mixed with trepidation. These he knows, and they know him; these belong to him, and he to them. As Lewis scholar Paul F. Ford has noted, Aslan in this scene acts less as a judge than as a witness, placing a seal on the judgments all moral beings have made for themselves.

Lewis's handling of this scene is very much in accord with his larger understanding of divine nature. Lewis recognized a certain tension between the traditional Christian doctrines of predestination and free will. In one letter, he described this conundrum as similar to the one physicists struggle with in trying to describe subatomic entities as waves or particles. But ultimately, Lewis asserted that the deepest spiritual truth is that of free will. God limits his sovereignty in order to allow souls genuine free choice in their daily lives and in their final destiny.

In the popular mind, Judgment Day is sometimes envisioned as a time of great and soul-shaking suspense. Subjects wait anxiously as some angelic auditor tabulates a lifetime of deeds, good and bad, like assets and debts on a ledger. If the good outweighs the bad, fortunate souls are rewarded with eternal bliss in some cloudy paradise. If not, they are banished to a place of much lower elevation and much higher temperature. Of course, this is not accurate Christian theology, and it is certainly not Lewis's understanding of the final reckoning. The apostle Paul explained to the believers at Ephesus that they were saved by grace through faith—a gift from God, not a reward for their own works.

Lewis took the Christian doctrine of salvation and applied it to each person's spiritual journey as a whole. In this view, heaven and hell are not just two possible destinations at the end of a lifetime; they are a soul's ongoing orientation throughout one's lifetime. In *Mere Christianity,* Lewis argued that Christian morality should not be seen as a kind of bargain with God in which he rewards those who follow the rules and punishes those who don't. Lewis believed, rather, that every choice we make reorients a central part of ourselves, so that we are not quite the same person as before the choice. Through a lifetime of choices, we are gradually shaping this central self into a heavenly creature, in harmony with God and others, or a hellish creature, in a perpetual war to defend the sovereignty of Self. Lewis concludes, "To be the one kind of creature is heaven: that is, it is joy and peace and knowledge and power. To be the other means madness, horror, rage, impotence, and eternal loneliness." Lewis's understanding of how all moral beings are ultimately responsible for their own final destiny is aptly illustrated in the closing pages of *The Last Battle*. The self-sorting of the Talking Beasts into paths of light or darkness also embodies Lewis's conviction, expressed in *The Great Divorce*: "There are only two kinds of people in the end: those who say to God, 'Thy will be done,' and those to whom God says, in the end, '*Thy* will be done.'"

In *The Last Battle,* this principle applies even to one who does not realize he has been following Aslan's will. Emeth, a Calormene soldier of noble birth, is a sincere seeker who has been faithfully trying to serve Tash all his life. When he enters the new Narnia and meets Aslan, he recognizes that the great lion "surpassed in beauty all that is in the world, even as the rose in bloom surpasses the dust of the desert." As a worshipper of Tash, Emeth assumes his hour of death has come, yet he feels "it is better to see the Lion and die" than to live and rule all of Calormen. But Aslan welcomes Emeth, explaining that all worthy service done for Tash is actually service done for Aslan.

This passage has made some theologically conservative readers uncomfortable, as it seems to suggest some sort of universalism on Lewis's part. But Lewis rejected both universalism and predestination as negations of free will. His position is better described as "inclusivism," the idea that Christ's reconciling work may sometimes apply even to those who are not aware of it. Lewis did not feel he was being unorthodox in this matter.

He referred several times in his letters to Christ's portrayal of judgment in which he welcomes those who fed the hungry, clothed the naked, and visited the sick, saying that all such service done for the least of his brethren is accounted as service done to him.

In addressing the larger problem of the "virtuous heathen" in *Mere Christianity,* Lewis argued that God never explained what his arrangements were for those who never heard the Gospel and had no chance to believe. He concluded, "We do know that no man can be saved except through Christ; we do not know that only those who know Him can be saved through Him." In a private letter written in 1952, Lewis made his conviction even more plain: "I think every prayer which is sincerely made even to a false god or to a very imperfectly conceived true God is accepted by the true God, and that Christ saves many who do not think they know him." The noble Emeth illustrates this principle, fulfilling as well Aslan's observation that "all find what they truly seek."

Cee

When a nine-year-old American boy named Laurence began to worry that he loved Aslan more than Christ, his mother wrote to Lewis in care of his publisher, Macmillan Publishing. Within ten days, she received a reassuring reply from Lewis himself, explaining that the Creator understands how a little boy's imagination works and isn't offended if a child is attracted to the image of God as a lion. Lewis asked for Laurence to pray, "If Mr. Lewis has worried any other children by his books or done them any harm, then please forgive him and help him never to do it again." Lewis also emphasized to Laurence's mother that "the things he loves Aslan for doing or saying are simply the things Jesus really did and said. So when Laurence thinks he is loving Aslan, he is really loving Jesus, and perhaps loving Him more than he ever did before."

As with Laurence, perhaps also with Lewis. George Sayer, Lewis's friend and biographer, believed that writing the Narnia stories was for Lewis an exercise in spiritual growth. Sayer wrote that "the Narnia stories reveal more about Jack's personal religion than any of his theological books, because he wrote them more from the heart than from the head." Another friend, Dom Bede Griffiths, heartily agreed: "The figure of Aslan tells us more of how Lewis understood the nature of God than anything else he wrote. It has all the hidden power and majesty and awesomeness which Lewis associated with God, but also all the glory and the tenderness and even the humor which he believed belonged to him, so that children could run up to him and throw their arms around him and kiss him. . . . It is 'Mere Christianity.'"

This sounds a bit like "Personal Heresy," Lewis's term for reading too much of an author's personal life into his or her books. But he probably would not have objected in this case. Sayer and Griffiths had both been students of his, then later companions on his walking tours and close personal friends. They knew the man well. And in his letters to children, Lewis sometimes used the name Aslan as a synonym for God.

For example, two years after writing a reassuring letter to Laurence's mother, Lewis wrote to Laurence himself, then eleven, about Joy Davidman Lewis's serious illness: "I am sure Aslan knows best and whether He leaves her with me or takes her to His own country, He will do what is right." From Lewis's letters and the observations of his friends, it would seem that Aslan's words to Lucy about learning to know him by another name applied to Lewis himself: "This was the very reason you were brought to Narnia, that by knowing me here for a little, you may know me better there."

CHAPTER FOUR

Moral Psychology

When all four Pevensie children arrive in Narnia together in *The Lion, the Witch and the Wardrobe*, they discover that Lucy's friend Tumnus has been arrested by the White Witch's secret police. As they are trying to decide what to do next, a bright-eyed robin gets their attention, beckoning them to follow him. Edmund isn't sure the robin ought to be trusted, saying the bird may be leading them into a trap. His older brother Peter considers this a moment, then answers, "Still—a robin you know. They're good birds in all the stories I've ever read. I'm sure a robin wouldn't be on the wrong side." Peter's instincts are sound; the redbreast is leading them to Mr. and Mrs. Beaver, followers of Aslan. It is Edmund himself who will turn out to be on the wrong side.

It may seem odd for a thoughtful young man like Peter to base his moral judgment on fantasy stories he's read. But in the world of Narnia, fairy tales, as well as old poems, are indeed reliable guides. Mr. Beaver quotes a rickety old rhyme that says the evil era will pass "When Adam's flesh and Adam's bone/ Sits at Cair Paravel in throne." The Pevensie children will eventually learn the truth of this prophecy and that they themselves are its fulfillment. Throughout the Narnia chronicles, good characters pay heed to nursery stories and rhymed messages, while evil characters ignore them. Both Caspian and Reepicheep turn out to be wise in believing their childhood nurses; but Miraz, the usurper in *Prince Caspian,* dismisses the idea of Talking Beasts as "fairy tales" and "nonsense . . . only fit for babies." He is wrong about this, and his mistake will eventually cost him his ill-gotten throne.

The chronicles themselves may also serve as faithful guides, illustrating moral failure and moral recovery. Lewis disagreed with the common complaint that fantasy stories are escapist; he felt they might just as easily be used to engage reality as to run away from it. In fact, he wrote in *Surprised by Joy* that children's stories are often less escapist than supposedly realistic juvenile fiction. After all, a child may enjoy a book like *Peter Rabbit* without wanting to become a rabbit. But a school story about the awkward novice who becomes a star varsity player appeals to the reader's actual fantasies and idle daydreams. The characters and setting of such a story may be realistic, but its outcome is pure escapist fantasy.

In the chronicles, Lewis adopted the opposite strategy from the school stories he disliked. He created a fantasy world that invites readers to consider the moral and psychological realities of *our* world. Lewis affirmed what he called the "doctrine of objective value, the belief that certain attitudes are really true, and others really false, to the kind of thing the universe is and the kinds of things we are." He believed there is a fabric of interwoven moral laws in the world that are just as universal and unalterable as the laws of the physical world. He called this the Tao, from the Chinese term for the Way, or the Road: "It is the Way in which the universe goes on, the Way in which things everlastingly emerge, stilly and tranquilly, into space and time. It is also the Way which everyone should tread in imitation of cosmic and supercosmic progression." In this view, a key element of moral education is teaching the young how to conform their wills to the Way, turning away from selfish or unworthy instincts toward the duties and responsibilities acknowledged in nearly all societies.

Contemporary fiction, even children's fiction, often stresses moral ambiguity, cultural relativism, and the difficulty of discerning good and evil. But Lewis believed there is a broad consensus among religious traditions about basic right and wrong, about the value of honesty, courage, and compassion. He considered moral relativism a "resounding lie," and included a twenty-five-page appendix in *The Abolition of Man,* quoting ethical teachings from many times and places that praise honesty, generosity, compassion, and respect for elders, while condemning violence, cruelty, greed, selfishness, dishonesty, or faithlessness to one's family.

Such broad definitions of right and wrong sound like a mere platitudes when stated in general terms. After all, everyone approves, in principle, of bravery over cowardice and compassion over selfishness. But the crucible of character is not moral precepts but actual moral choices, situations where the right decision is not the easiest or the safest one. In the world of Narnia, all the major characters are faced with such choices, and readers are allowed to learn along with them.

Edmund's Moral Descent

In general, Lewis's good characters and his bad ones are not hard to distinguish, and their moral qualities remain fairly constant. Lucy Pevensie probably comes the nearest to being a saint— consistently gentle, honest, brave, and compassionate. At the other end of the moral spectrum is that "old sinner" Andrew Ketterley, the would-be magician who is incorrigibly egocentric, cruel, cowardly, dishonest, and sometimes delusional.

The most interesting psychological cases in the chronicles are those who do not remain fixed in character but are profoundly changed by their time in Narnia. Perhaps the best example is Edmund Pevensie, who sinks down to what Dante considered one of the worst of sins—betrayal of kindred—and then recovers in later life so fully that he earns his title, Edmund the Just. By tracing Edmund's fall and rise, readers can see most of the qualities Lewis associated with moral malaise and moral health.

Lucy feels Edmund began to go wrong during his first term at a "horrid school." As noted earlier, Lewis used the term *childhood* in all his books to suggest simplicity, wonder, and self-forgetfulness. By contrast, he associated the terms *boyhood* and *school* with a time of life "in which everything (ourselves included) has been greedy, cruel, noisy, and prosaic, in which the imagination has slept." In 1962, nearly a half century after he left them behind, Lewis still described two of the boarding schools he attended (Wynyard and Malvern) as "very horrid" and said he hated them even worse than his time in the trenches of World War I. It is not surprising, then, that when we first meet Edmund in *The Lion, the Witch and the Wardrobe,* his time at boarding school has already turned him into a cynic and a bully.

There is very little to like about Edmund in the early pages of *The Lion, the Witch and the Wardrobe*. He laughs at Professor Kirke's eccentric looks, snaps at his older sister Susan when she says it's time for bed, and whines about a rainy day. He teases Lucy mercilessly about her "imaginary" world inside the wardrobe, not in fun but out of sheer spite. When Edmund gets into Narnia himself, he is easy prey for the blandishments of the White Witch. Her flattery appeals to his pride and her magical Turkish Delight to his gluttony. And her promise to make him a king appeals to his rebellious instinct to rule his older brother Peter, the natural leader of the family. By the time the evil queen sends Edmund back to his own world, her magic has already found a receptive vessel, and she has found in him a useful new vassal.

Lewis's concept of the central self (discussed in Chapter Three) affected one way or the other by every moral choice, implies a kind of moral momentum. Every good choice strengthens one's inner resolve to make another good choice next time, while every bad choice leaves one inclined to further bad choices down the road. At first, Edmund is only selfish and ill-tempered. But when he deliberately lies, refusing to confirm Lucy's story and admit there really is a magic world inside the wardrobe, he does great harm to his own soul. Here is falsehood, pride, and spite all bound up together, a sign that Edmund's downward drift has turned into a descent. Lewis wrote that "rebellion of the will" usually leads to "fogging of the intelligence," and Edmund's lie will lead to a whole series of wrong-headed and wrong-hearted choices.

When all four Pevensies discover Narnia together, Peter immediately turns to Lucy and says he's sorry for not believing her the first time. But Edmund pretends he's never been there before, showing how one lie so often leads to others. Then he slips up, pointing out the way to the lamppost, exposing himself as a liar and someone who put Lucy through needless misery. This moment would be an excellent time to apologize. But asking for forgiveness calls for both honesty and humility, two qualities Edmund lacks. So he only makes things worse by muttering to himself something about his siblings as "self-satisfied prigs." From that point on, his moral instincts are increasingly corrupted. He cares more about dinner than about helping Mr. Tumnus; he distrusts the robin and the beavers and keeps trying to convince himself that the imperious lady on the sledge might not be evil after all.

Edmund's moral state becomes especially clear when Mr. and Mrs. Beaver begin telling the Pevensies all about Narnia. When the four children hear the beaver say, "Aslan is on the move," they have no idea who or what Aslan is. Yet the very name has a mystical aura, laying bare the very soul of each one who hears it. The word makes Peter, the eldest, feel "brave and adventurous." His sister Susan feels as if "some delicious smell or delightful strain of music had just floated by her." For the youngest, Lucy, it is like waking up to discover the summer holidays have begun. For Edmund, though, the very name *Aslan* induces "a sensation of mysterious horror."

Throughout the chronicles, the surest gauge of a character's spiritual health is his or her response to Aslan. In *The Magician's Nephew*, Digory begins to hear the voice of the lion singing Narnia into existence, and he finds it "beyond comparison, the most beautiful noise he ever heard." Frank the cabby has a similar response, exclaiming, "Glory be! I'd ha' been a better man all my life if I'd known there were things like this." But while the cabby and the children drink in the sound with their eyes glistening, Uncle Andrew's knees shake, and he thinks he would rather crawl in a rat hole than keep listening to this voice. Jadis the Witch is also repelled by the sound. She senses in it a magic stronger than her own and wishes she could smash this new world to pieces to silence that voice. When the lion himself appears, Andrew wants to shoot him with a gun, and Jadis throws an iron bar at him. (The bar is the crosspiece she has ripped off a London lamppost. It bounces harmlessly off Aslan's head, and in those fertile moments of Narnia's creation, it grows into a whole lamppost. Thus Lewis solved the problem of how a lamppost came to be standing all by itself in the wilds of Narnia!)

In *Mere Christianity,* Lewis defined pride as "the complete anti-God state of mind." In the chronicles, it is the prideful characters, the ones who would be gods unto themselves, who are most repelled by Aslan, who wish to escape his presence. Jadis and Andrew are a pair of villains, so of course they want to get as far away as possible from supreme goodness. But the same pattern emerges even among the middling characters of Narnia. In *The Horse and His Boy,* when Aslan first appears to two Narnian horses, Bree and Hwin, their responses are quite revealing. Bree, the proud warhorse, is so startled that he bolts away and doesn't look back until he comes to a wall too high for jumping. The usually timid Hwin, however, trots toward the great lion, not away from him. Though shaking, she tells Aslan he's so beautiful that she would rather be devoured by him than fed by anyone else. "Dearest daughter," he answers, "Joy shall be yours."

Though Bree overcomes his initial shock and reins in his pride before Aslan, Edmund has a good deal further to go before his foolish conceit is shattered. Seeming to want to escape the very name of Aslan, he slips away from the others, headed for the White Witch's castle. The narrator explains that Edmund doesn't wish any actual harm to the others; he's just full of silly ideas about getting more magic candy and being made a king and paying back his older brother. He tells himself the queen can't be as bad as all that, though "deep down inside him he really knew the White Witch was bad and cruel." Edmund began his downward descent by lying to the others about Narnia as a real place. Now he has begun to lie to himself.

Honesty

In Narnia, honesty is not only the best policy; it is also the best therapy. Genuine moral and mental health consists not only in telling the truth to others but also in telling the truth to oneself about one's true interests and motives. As Edmund treads through the snow to the White Witch's house, he hears more than one voice inside. One is telling him that he is making a great mistake, that he needs to turn back, to repent. But it is drowned out by other voices crying "I want" and "I deserve" and "I'll show them."

Throughout the chronicles, characters cannot experience genuine moral growth until they learn to hear the still, small voice of truth within them, ignoring the inner clamor of evasions and rationalizations. Sometimes Aslan himself plays the part of counselor, coaxing characters into speaking the simple truth. In *The Silver Chair,* he asks Jill Pole why she stood so near the edge of the cliff from which Eustace fell. "I was showing off,

Sir," Jill explains candidly, to which Aslan replies, "That is a very good answer." Confirming that she is clear on that point, Aslan goes on to explain to Jill the mission for which he called her to Narnia. But he wants her to understand at the outset that her own behavior has already made the task more difficult.

In a similar situation in *The Magician's Nephew,* Aslan asks Digory Kirke how the evil Jadis found her way into Narnia. Digory begins to explain that he met the witch on a world called Charn, but Aslan interrupts, "You *met* the Witch?" Digory explains more clearly that the witch woke up, then even more clearly that he awoke her by ringing a bell. He knew at the time that it was a wrong thing to do, but now he says he wonders aloud if he might have been enchanted by the writing under the bell. "Do you?" asks Aslan, in a low voice. Digory admits that he wasn't enchanted but was only pretending to be. Ultimately, he is forced to acknowledge that his own willfulness brought evil into Narnia. Only after this candid confession can Aslan proceed, saying that he will ensure that the evil consequences of the boy's rash act will not fall on Digory but upon himself.

Technology

Aslan's comment in *The Magician's Nephew* that he would take the evil upon himself is a prophecy, one that is fulfilled when he takes Edmund's place on the Stone Table in *The Lion, the Witch and the Wardrobe.* But Edmund has no idea what forces he has set into motion as he trudges through the snow, planning to betray his brother and sisters to the White Witch. Instead, his head is full of idle thoughts about what he'll do when he becomes king

of Narnia, how he'll pass some new laws against beavers and find
ways to keep Peter in his place. Edmund also decides that as
king, he'll put in some decent roads, plus a railway system. He
dreams as well about his luxurious palace, all the fancy cars he'll
have, and his own private cinema.

Readers with even a passing acquaintance of C. S. Lewis
will recognize at once that a character with such daydreams
floating through his head has become confused about the qualities of a life well lived. Lewis preferred simple, old-fashioned
things, and he often complained about the modern world's preoccupation with luxury and technology. He favored walking to
riding in a car because, he said, a vehicle "annihilates space." He
disliked radio, television, and cinema and didn't even recognize
the names of major movie stars of his generation. (Two of the
very few films he went to see, and enjoyed, were fantasy stories—*Snow White* and *King Kong.*) In *Out of the Silent Planet,* Lewis
refers to the blighted history of earth in terms of its "wars and
industrialisms," as if the two could be considered twin curses.
In the chronicles as well, it is the evil characters who are always
thinking about technology and industrial development. After
witnessing the creation of Narnia, Andrew
exclaims that "the commercial possibilities of this country are un-
bounded." He starts babbling about
creating railway engines and battle-
ships out of scrap iron, about starting
health resorts and sanatoriums,
which will make him millions. Shift
the Ape in *The Last Battle* has a similar vision. He says he'll make Narnia

"a country worth living in" by importing oranges and bananas, by building "roads and big cities and schools and offices," not to mention everything needed to subdue animals—"whips and muzzles and saddles and cages and kennels." Like Andrew at the beginning of Narnia and Shift at its end, Edmund's vision for an industrialized Narnia clearly reveals him to be far from the author's own sympathies.

Empathy

Edmund finally reaches the witch's palace after dark, stopping to pencil a beard and glasses on a stone lion he thinks might be Aslan turned to a statue by the queen's sorcery. This is a symbolic desecration of the one whose name had filled him with horror; it is also an act of mean-spirited schoolboy vandalism. Yet there is something stirring in Edmund that is about to awaken. Even as he tries to take pleasure at mocking the stone lion, he senses something "terrible and sad and noble" on that face staring up in the moonlight.

When he meets the witch again, Edmund finds out immediately what a fool he has been. Instead of giving him more Turkish Delight, she gives him a crust of dry bread and tells him he's lucky to have even that. Instead of making him a prince, she treats him like a prisoner. As she sets out on her sledge to find the other children, she drags him along in the cold, dispelling any last illusions he might have had about her being a good queen. On the way there, she encounters a merry family of squirrels and their friends, celebrating a visit from Father Christmas with an outdoor feast. She is enraged by this hint that her power is slipping away, and she raises her wand, turning them all to stone.

When Edmund pleads with her to spare them, she strikes him hard across the face. At this point, he is cold, hungry, bruised, bone weary, and clearly the hostage of an evil sorceress. If ever he had good reason to indulge in self-pity, this would be the time. Yet we learn from the narrator that "Edmund for the first time in this story felt sorry for someone besides himself." He couldn't help but think of those poor creatures turned to stone, frozen in place for all those days and nights until at last their features crumbled to dust. (One of Lewis's readers also worried about these poor creatures whose festivity was turned to statuary. When she wrote and asked about them, Lewis replied that they had all returned to normal at the same time that Aslan later rescued the others who had been turned to stone.

The dormant pity that Edmund felt for the stone lion in the witch's courtyard now fully awakens. This is the first clear sign that Edmund's moral regeneration has begun. Miserable as he is himself, Edmund feels compassion for others. Apart from their direct response to Aslan himself, the clearest way to discern the moral health of a character in Narnia is to note which ones think of others and which ones think only of themselves. In *The Screwtape Letters,* Lewis wrote that the very mark of hell is a "ruthless, sleepless, unsmiling concentration on the self." Early in the story, Edmund had such a mark upon him when he thought a rainy day was a good excuse to feel sorry for himself. But having undergone real suffering, having endured the painful consequences of his own choices, Edmund finally discovers what it means to care about others.

In nearly all the chronicles, Lewis includes at least one scene that contrasts one character's unblinking selfishness with another's simple concern for others. Both Uncle Andrew and Queen Jadis in *The Magician's Nephew* spout grand nonsense about their "high and lonely destiny," while Digory and Polly feel sorry for the animals and ordinary people whose lives are destroyed by such talk. When the princess Aravis in *The Horse and His Boy* explains her clever scheme of escape by drugging a slave girl, Shasta is less impressed by the stratagem than he is worried about how the slave girl will be punished. In the Narnia stories, some characters, like Lucy, are born kind; some, like Edmund, achieve kindness; and some, like Aravis, have kindness thrust upon them.

In his nightmarish journey on the queen's sledge, Edmund not only begins to see other people in a new way but also begins to see Nature with new eyes. With Aslan's coming, the long witch's winter is nearing an end and spring arrives, not week by week but minute by minute. Even though his hands are tied and he is being dragged along on foot, Edmund can't help but see patches of green grass and spring flowers and hear the burbling of brook water and the chirping of birds. The narrator explains that Edmund's heart gives "a great leap" when he realizes the frost is ending. The phrasing here recalls the famous poem by William Wordsworth that begins, "My heart leaps up when I behold a rainbow in the sky." Wordsworth was one of Lewis's favorite poets, someone who shared with Lewis a deep sense of joy and gratitude in the beauty of the natural world. Only the day before, Edmund had been thinking about the roads and railways he would build in Narnia, about cars and cities and cinemas. That he is now attending to budding birches and blooming celandines is another sign that Edmund's spiritual recovery is well under way.

Privacy

Just as the witch prepares to cut Edmund's throat, he is saved by a rescue party sent by Aslan. Edmund is carried off to meet the great lion and to be reunited with his brother and sisters. Aslan's first meeting with Edmund, and their conversation, might have been one of the climactic scenes of the story. But the other children see the lion and the little boy walking off by themselves, and no one hears what words pass between them. We are only told "it was a conversation which Edmund never forgot" and that he came back, shook hands, and said "I'm sorry" to each of the others. What would Aslan say to a boy who has betrayed his family and for whom the lion is planning to lay down his own life? The others never find out, and neither do the readers.

This is a recurring motif in the Narnia chronicles. Whenever characters want to know what will happen to another or what might have happened, Aslan turns aside their curiosity. When Lucy asks in *The Voyage of the "Dawn Treader"* if Eustace will be allowed to return to Narnia, Aslan answers, "Child, do you really need to know that?" In *The Horse and His Boy,* when Aravis, with belated compassion, asks if any further harm will come to the slave girl she drugged, the lion replies, "I am telling you your story, not hers." He seems to want each person to focus on his or her own life, not to compare themselves with others or wonder what might have been. Aslan's dismissal of idle curiosity recalls an incident in the Gospel of John, where one disciple, Peter, asks Jesus what will become of another disciple, John. "What is that to thee?" their master replies, and then says, "Follow thou me." Lewis quoted this verse in *Mere Christianity* as a caution about asking questions that tantalize the mind without feeding the soul.

Whatever Aslan said to Edmund was all that needed to be said. In the final confrontation with the witch and her army, it is Edmund's insight and bravery that turn the tide of battle. He fights his way to the witch and smashes her wand, recognizing it as her chief source of power. Edmund's bravery in battle is yet another sign that he has recovered his true self. In the chronicles, courage does not mean immunity from fear; it is overcoming fear. When Edmund's brother goes to rescue Susan from the jaws of Maugrim the wolf, the narrator explains: "Peter did not feel very brave; indeed, he felt he was going to be sick. But that made no difference to what he had to do." In all the Narnia stories, the protagonists have to set aside their fears in order to do what has to be done. This is more an act of moral courage than physical courage. As Lewis noted in *The Screwtape Letters,* "Courage is not simply *one* of the virtues, but the form of every virtue at the testing point. . . . A chastity or honesty or mercy which yields to danger will be chaste or honest or merciful on conditions. Pilate was merciful till it became risky."

Edmund accepts the risks in the final battle with the witch, and he is severely wounded. But Lucy's healing potion restores him to his old self again, his *real* old self from before he had gone off to school and been spoiled. The Pevensie children go on to become kings and queens of Narnia, and the younger brother, fully restored, becomes known as Edmund the Just.

Trust

When the four Pevensie children return to Narnia in *Prince Caspian* (the sequel to *The Lion, the Witch and the Wardrobe* as the books were originally published), readers cannot help but wonder if Edmund's old character defects will return. When the children are called back, they find that in the one year they were back on earth, many centuries have passed in Narnia. Arriving amid the overgrown ruins of their old castle, Cair Paravel, they have to wend their way cross-country to join a band of Old Narnians, led by the rightful heir to the throne, young Caspian, fighting his conniving uncle Miraz. As the Pevensies, led by the loyal dwarf Trumpkin, are trying to make their way across rugged terrain, Lucy sees Aslan on an uphill slope, when the others are making their way down. She tries to persuade the others that they're going the wrong way, but no one else saw anything out of the ordinary.

In a magnanimous gesture, Edmund takes Lucy at her word, even in the absence of other evidence. This is a poignant example of spiritual healing. For this is the same Edmund who pretended not to believe Lucy in *The Lion, the Witch and the Wardrobe,* even though he had seen Narnia with his own eyes. In *Prince Caspian,* Edmund the Just becomes also Edmund the Trusting, believing even when he cannot see. Later in the story, Aslan will reward this trust by welcoming Edmund with the words "Well done."

Edmund remains a strong character in *The Voyage of the "Dawn Treader,"* one who helps his cousin Eustace Scrubb learn many of the same lessons he himself has learned. Like Edmund, Eustace starts out as a selfish whiner, spoiled not by school but by his "progressive" parents. But he too suffers and learns, discovering how to care for others besides himself and even how to be brave. When Eustace apologizes late in the story for his beastly behavior, Edmund reassures him: "That's all right. Between ourselves, you haven't been as bad as I was on my first trip to Narnia. You were only an ass, but I was a traitor." When Eustace asks, "But who is Aslan? Do you know him?" Edmund answers wisely, "Well—he knows me."

Like Edmund, Eustace's change for the better will be permanent, and he will measure up to his mission when he returns to Narnia in *The Silver Chair*. In the chronicles, Lewis depicts good and bad characters, as well as morally weak characters turning into strong ones. But nowhere does he present morally strong characters lapsing into evil. They may have brief moments of weakness, but Lewis's good characters always regain their moral equilibrium before too long. Unlike J.R.R. Tolkien's fiction, which presents moral decline as an ever-present danger, Lewis's fiction suggests that ethical foundations, once properly laid, will stand firm on the day of testing.

Of course, Lewis didn't write the chronicles to be manuals on morals. When one child wrote Lewis, saying she didn't like "silly adventure stories without any point," he wasn't sure if he agreed. He thought if a story was silly, then having a point wouldn't save it, but if it was good in itself, it might not need a point. He thought readers might lose the full effect of a story if they looked too hard for a moral. Then he admitted he hadn't fully made up his mind about this whole issue. But he agreed that the point of a story would be "some truth about the real world which one can take out of it." Lewis's own Narnia stories pass the test on both counts. They are good in themselves, even for those not seeking a point. But for others, reading the chronicles is not a means of escaping the "real world" but rather a means of embracing it more fully.

CHAPTER FIVE

Classical and Medieval Elements

C. S. Lewis was a renowned medieval and Renaissance scholar who didn't believe in the Renaissance. When he was first invited to give a series of lectures on the subject at Cambridge, he thought of calling his lectures "Absence of the Renaissance." For an alternate title, he considered, "What Was Happening While the Renaissance Was Not Taking Place." To a distinguished fellow scholar, Douglas Bush of Harvard University, Lewis defined the Renaissance as "an imaginary entity responsible for anything a modern writer approves of in the fifteenth or sixteenth century."

Of course, Lewis knew there was an era called the Renaissance by later generations, a time of revived interest in Greek and Latin texts, expanding scientific knowledge, and increasing secularization. But he considered the term *Renaissance*, "rebirth," a gross overstatement, as a "dead" civilization does not produce classics of Arthurian romance, a poetic genius such as Dante, or cathedrals such as those at Chartres and Canterbury.

Lewis's whole person was drawn to a time when Western civilization could with some accuracy be called Christendom and when a predominant literary form was epic romance. The world of Aquinas and King Arthur, of Boethius and Beowulf, was the world in which Lewis the scholar, the Christian, and the lover of heroic adventure could feel most at home. In his scholarly works such as *The Allegory of Love* and *The Discarded Image,* Lewis carefully explained the world-picture that dominated Western culture for a thousand years. In the Chronicles of Narnia, he seeks to recover parts of that image for modern readers.

The usual outline, still found in many history books, is that ancient Greece and Rome achieved the first summit in Western civilization—the classical era. Then came a hiatus lasting for centuries, the so-called Dark Ages and Middle Ages. (Even the term *medieval* means nothing more than "middle era.") Finally, the cultural stagnation was overcome by the humanists, who awakened a slumbering glory and began the ascent to a new cultural summit.

Lewis found this common view of Western civilization presumptuous and misleading. He denied that the medieval era represented a radical break with the classical era and that the Renaissance represented a radical break with the Middle Ages. The "Great Divide," he argued, came in the revolution of the nineteenth and twentieth centuries, creating an industrialized, post-Christian era that divides the modern world from previous generations more than any of them are separated from one another.

Rather than accepting that there was a fundamental shift between the classical world and the Christian era, Lewis consistently stressed the continuity between the pagan and the

Christian. In *The Discarded Image,* for example, he spends two pages showing that pagans and early Christians had far more in common than either shares with modern thinkers. *Pagan* is one of those words, like *childhood* and *nurse,* that has a specialized meaning in Lewis's books. In common usage, *pagan* and *Christian* are practically contraries, the first representing a secular, this-worldly attitude, and the second representing its opposite. Lewis saw no such antithesis; he called paganism "the childhood of religion . . . a prophetic dream." For him, paganism was an anticipation, Christianity the fulfillment.

In so defining his terms, Lewis is revealing personal history as well as his reading of cultural history. Lewis began learning Latin from his mother in the idyllic years before he was sent off to boarding school. He associated paganism with myth and romance, and Christianity with the reality that myth and romance point to. Just as his own love of classic texts was fulfilled when he reaffirmed his childhood faith, he saw the highest strivings of paganism fulfilled with the coming of the Christian era. As he later explained it to a childhood friend, "I think the thrill of the Pagan stories and of romance may be due to the fact that they are mere beginnings—the first, faint whisper of the wind from beyond the world—while Christianity is the thing itself."

Lewis's attitude is just as evident in his fiction as in his scholarly books. Some readers who have heard the chronicles described as Christian fantasy are surprised to find the world of Narnia peopled with fauns, satyrs, tree nymphs, and even specific Roman gods such as Bacchus, god of wine and revelry, and Pomona, goddess of orchards. But Lewis believed that the noblest classical myths represented "a real though unfocused gleam of divine truth falling on human imagination." His created world is full of biblical echoes and teachings, but it is also a cornucopia of creatures from myth, legend, and folklore—centaurs, dragons, dwarves, giants, gnomes, and so on. In his scholarly books, Lewis noted with approval how medieval and Elizabethan authors freely mixed classical and Christian elements in their creative works. In the chronicles, he decided to revive this practice in modern-day children's stories.

Just as he stressed the continuity between the classical and the Christian, Lewis also stressed the continuity between the medieval era and the Renaissance. He described the notion of the "medieval" as a fifteenth-century humanistic invention that dismissed "a thousand years of theology, metaphysics, jurisprudence, courtesy, poetry, and architecture . . . as a mere gap or chasm." He avoided the term *Renaissance* because he considered it an empty term of self-congratulation invented by the same humanists, one that imposed a false unity on a diverse assortment of cultural events. The influence of Lewis's new understanding of Western culture was already evident in his lifetime, when Magdalene College, Cambridge, created especially for him the position of professor of medieval and Renaissance literature. In accepting the position, Lewis applauded the title "Medieval *and* Renaissance," asserting that "the barrier between those two

ages has been greatly exaggerated, if indeed it was not largely a figment of Humanist propaganda."

Lewis devoted a great deal of his energy

and expertise as a scholar to the task of rehabilitating the medieval worldview, urging his readers to recognize the intellectual and artistic achievements of writers who might otherwise have been considered mainly as forerunners. For example, he pointed out in several of his scholarly books that medieval authors did not believe the earth was flat; they knew our world to be a globe. He also quoted several medieval philosophers, showing that they realized the earth was a tiny speck in comparison to the vastness of the universe.

In writing the chronicles, Lewis's task was not to argue for the intellectual vitality of the medieval worldview but rather to show its imaginative beauty. In all the Narnia books, Lewis includes a wealth of details to suggest what the medieval vision of reality might have felt like from the inside.

Hierarchy

When King Caspian reclaims the Lone Islands for the realm of Narnia in *The Voyage of the "Dawn Treader,"* he dismisses a corrupt bureaucrat named Gumpas. But Caspian does not call for free and fair elections, nor does he consult local leaders about Gumpas's successor. Rather, he simply says, "I think we have had enough of governors," and names his friend Lord Bern the new ruler, proclaiming him Duke of the Lone Islands. In Narnia, the preferred form of government is not democracy but enlightened monarchy.

Lewis was pragmatic enough to advocate democracy for the contemporary world, not because people are good enough to deserve it but because they are so prone to abuse power that it needs to be spread out. Nonetheless, democracy seemed to him, like so much else about the contemporary world, prosaic and utilitarian when compared with the grandeur and elegance of earlier eras. He complained about modern "Govertisement," government by advertisement, the increasing trend for leaders to be marketed the same way as shaving cream. He also noted that earlier eras sought out *rulers,* those who kept the peace and who governed with diligence and integrity. He contrasted this with the modern ideal of a *leader,* someone with "dash" and "magnetism" who deliberately orchestrates "drives" and "campaigns" in order to stir up mass excitement. Clearly, Lewis preferred the older view of governance.

Lewis also explained that older conceptions of social hierarchy were linked to people's view of the cosmic hierarchy. From ancient times until the Enlightenment, people viewed the universe as the Great Chain of Being, with God at the top of the cosmic order and unformed matter at the bottom. Everyone and everything had a natural station, ruling over those below, obeying those above. A great many sins, according to this view, derive from not recognizing one's position, thus perverting the natural order.

In *A Preface to Paradise Lost,* Lewis listed the most common distortions of the natural order as tyranny (trying to rule one's equals), servility (being ruled by equals), rebellion (disobeying one's superiors), and remissness (failing in one's duty to rule over one's subjects). In this view, the first great disruption in the cosmic order was the revolt of Lucifer, an act of rebellion against the absolutely Supreme, God himself. Then came the fall of Adam, a double sin of not obeying God and (in Milton's view) not ruling over his wife Eve.

In the chronicles, most evil or misguided acts are sins against the natural order of Narnia. After destroying her home world of Charn, Jadis becomes a tyrant in trying to rule Narnia by force. Part of Edmund's temptation in *The Lion, the Witch and the Wardrobe* is to rule over his older brother Peter and his other siblings. As the younger brother, this is not his place. Throughout that book, Peter, the eldest, is portrayed as the natural leader of the family. He is the one who takes the problem of Lucy's Narnia "delusions" to Professor Kirke, and he is quick to apologize when he sees that she was telling the truth. He is first to approach the awe-inspiring Aslan, realizing it is his duty as the eldest. And despite his inner fears, he fights and kills Fenris (Maugrim), the evil wolf.

The Voyage of the "Dawn Treader" illustrates several ways in which the social order can be disrupted. The Lone Islands have ceased to pay tribute to the king, so Caspian deposes its governor and installs a duke. On Coriakin's island, the foolish Monopods refuse to obey their natural ruler and have to be controlled by "rough magic." (Unlike their unruly but comical cousins, the treacherous dwarves in *The Last Battle* provide a much more serious example of rebellion.) Near the end of the tale, Caspian falls prey to the error of remissness. It is all right for Reepicheep to seek out Aslan's country, because he is a knight errant (or in this case, a knight rodent). But when King Caspian wants to follow the same quest, his fellow voyagers react with dismay. Rynelf the sailor tells him that's little better than desertion, and Drinian the captain calls it abdicating. Reepicheep is most eloquent of all, explaining to Caspian, "You are the King of Narnia. You break faith with all your subjects . . . if you do not return. You shall not please yourself with adventures as if you were a private person." Looking for a moment like his evil old uncle Miraz, Caspian goes into a sulk, and it takes a visit from Aslan himself to help the king remember his duty to others.

Of course, there is a danger in emphasizing too much the necessity of knowing one's place, of accepting one's station in the social order. In our world, there has been a great deal of harm done by the idea that certain people are naturally superior to others, that some are born to rule simply because of their bloodline, not because of their merits. But Lewis made clear that he saw the necessity of democracy in our world, that aristocracy would only work in a better world than ours. For example, the first king of Narnia is not some heir of Arthur or Charlemagne called from our world. He is a humble, brave, devout Cockney cabbie, someone whose responsibilities, as defined by Aslan, are to till the earth, to rule Narnia's creatures kindly and fairly, to lead in battle, and to raise children with the same qualities.

Chivalry

Lewis's two main literary delights in his childhood were stories about "dressed animals" and "knights in armor." Sometimes he combined these into tales of his own about chivalrous mice and rabbits. When he began writing for children forty years later, the charm of these stories had not faded. Narnia is a world of knights and chivalry, dances and pageants, courtesy and fair speech.

Lewis's enthusiasm for chivalric romance was one of the constants of his life. Even as a teenager, when he had set aside his childhood faith and what he considered childish reading, young Lewis was devouring texts for his own pleasure that many graduate students nowadays find difficult. At the age of sixteen, he pronounced Malory's *Morte D'Arthur* (1485) "the greatest thing I've ever read," adding that its phrasing bore a "sweet breath from the old-time, faery world." The next year he read the fourteenth-century Arthurian poem *Sir Gawain and the Green Knight* and said its only flaw was that it is too short. In the same month (May 1916), he read a medieval French version of the Tristan and Iseult story, as well as Chaucer's "Knight's Tale" (c. 1387), which he pronounced "the perfect poem of chivalry."

Having immersed himself in so many tales of adventure and enchantment, the young Lewis decided that same year it was time for him to try his own hand at it. He composed a sixty-four-page fragment called "The Quest of Bleheris" about a young man who feels the need to go on a heroic quest to win the hand of one Lady Alice. He considers various missions—to bind the "Lady of the Hideous Pass"; to visit the people who live underground, between earth and hell; or perhaps to seek the Well of Youth in the "uttermost lands" in the East. Though Bleheris chooses none of these quests, Lewis's Narnian characters, created more than thirty years later, will not neglect the opportunity. The Chronicles of Narnia contain three separate evil ladies, or witches (or perhaps the same one in three different incarnations), who must be bound. In *The Silver Chair,* Eustace, Jill, and Puddleglum journey far underground to rescue Prince Rilian. And the ultimate quest in *The Voyage of the "Dawn Treader,"* of course, is to seek out the utter East.

But the magnet for Bleheris's imagination is the North. He decides to cross the Great Mountains in search of a mysterious figure called Striver, whom some consider a monster but others revere as a god. On the way, he meets a dreamy young man named Wan Jadis, who says he is in search of the land of Yesterday. He describes this as a place of misty valleys and fluttering golden leaves where one might meet legendary queens such as Helen of Troy or Guinevere. Wan Jadis tries to lead Bleheris to the place of Yesterday but ends up drowning in a vermin-infested marsh. His foolish quest leads him not to the romantic past but to destruction. Perhaps with this character, Lewis was warning himself not to become so infatuated with an idealized Yesterday that he ceased to be grounded in Today.

Wan Jadis, whose name combines the English word for "pale" with the French adjective for "times of yore," is one whose search for Joy has become effete and sentimental. The young Lewis abandoned his story soon after the death of the likable but misguided Wan Jadis. Though Lewis never created a character quite like him in any of his published works, he kept the name Jadis for the powerful witch in *The Magician's Nephew*. This Jadis is nothing like the pallid aesthete in Lewis's early story, yet she too comes from a world where death prevails.

Though Lewis never finished his tale of Bleheris, his interest in chivalric romance continued throughout his lifetime. Apart from the medieval texts he never tired of reading, Lewis admired the historical narratives of Sir Walter Scott and William Morris. His book-length narrative poem *Dymer* (1926) features an evil enchanter, and his spiritual allegory *Pilgrim's Regress* (1933) pictures Reason as a woman clad in armor, freeing captives with her quick sword and quicker wits. In 1948, Lewis

published *Arthurian Torso,* a fragment on Camelot by his deceased
friend Charles Williams, along with
Lewis's commentary on Williams's
Arthurian poems.

It is not surprising, then, that
chivalry is not dead in the world of
Narnia. Though there are kings or
knights in all the chronicles, the
most explicit chivalric elements
occur in the first three books published. The first appearance of
Aslan in *The Lion, the Witch and the Wardrobe,* for example, is
almost a medieval tableau. The Pevensie children see first a royal
pavilion of yellow silk with crimson cords and a waving banner
depicting a "red rampant lion." In heraldry, the word *rampant*
denotes an animal rearing up on its hind legs. As for the lion
himself, he is portrayed before a crowd of naiads, dryads, and
centaurs, with a leopard on either side of him, one holding a
crown and the other a standard. This scene, a lion between two
leopards holding his emblems of authority, is a common device
on medieval coats of arms. In their first sight of Aslan, the children have walked into a world of medieval pageantry and heraldry.

Perhaps the most striking chivalric scene in *Prince Caspian*
is Peter Pevensie's single combat with the usurper Miraz. Again,
this episode illustrates the importance of hierarchy. Miraz is
guilty of tyranny, seeking to rule over others as if he were king;
Peter, as the eldest and the High King, is the one whose duty it
is to throw down the gauntlet. In his formal challenge to Miraz,

Peter uses florid and archaic language like that of an Arthurian romance. Summarizing the usurpers' misdeeds, Peter insists on spelling the word *abominable* as "ad-hominable," which is the Middle English form. This spelling is based on a folk etymology meaning "away from human," behaving without conscience, like a wild beast. Peter also refers to single combat with the antiquated word *monomachy,* literally "one-strife."

Throughout the chronicles, Lewis uses archaic language to contribute to the atmosphere of medieval romance. The confluence of rivers is called a "waters-meet." A misbehaving boy is a "heart's-scald." The use of older words is especially noticeable at the end of *The Lion, the Witch and the Wardrobe,* when the Pevensie children, now kings and queens who have lived long in Narnia, converse in speech that sounds like mock Malory. They begin sentences with "Fair consorts," or "Marry," and they use outmoded verbs such as *worketh* and *stirreth.*

This sort of formal, courteous speech can seem like parody if it goes on too long. In the chapters portraying Edmund and Susan in *The Horse and His Boy,* they use the word *naught* for "naughty," and they refer to a royal tournament with the obscure old word *hastilude,* "spear play." But in general, their conversation in the later book is not nearly as stilted as in the last chapter of *The Lion, the Witch and the Wardrobe.* Lewis probably realized that a dash of archaism spiced up the dialogue but a full serving would soon spoil the discourse.

If the formal, courteous speech of chivalry is diminished when spoken by modern schoolchildren, even in Narnia, then why not put it in the mouth of a diminutive character? Lewis considered the mouse Reepicheep to be one of his most memorable creations in the chronicles. Surely, it is an inspired touch to embody the ideal of medieval knighthood in a furry, foot-tall package. It might sound pompous or grandiloquent for a battle-smeared warrior to say, "I am confounded. I am completely out of countenance. I must crave your indulgence for appearing in this unseemly fashion." But if the speaker is a proud, well-spoken mouse who has lost his tail, the speech sounds charmingly apt.

Lewis considered the ideal of knighthood, someone taking up arms in defense of a worthy cause, to be "one of the great Christian ideas." In the chronicles, this chivalric ideal is best embodied in Reepicheep. In addition to his agile swordsmanship and ever-courteous speech, it is Reepicheep who comforts Eustace, the boy-turned-dragon, with stories of Fortune's wheel, a medieval commonplace about how easily the high may be brought low but also how the fortunes of those in distress may be mended. And of course, Reepicheep's longing to find Aslan's country is a kind of grail quest. Lewis noted to a friend that the radiance and sweet fragrance of Aslan are qualities he recalled from reading descriptions of the Holy Grail.

People sometimes talk about the age of chivalry, as if there were actually some lost era in which the leaders of society were all governed by the dictates of honor, courage, civility, and courtesy. Lewis knew better. Writing about the Arthurian romances of the twelfth-century French poet Chrétien de Troyes, Lewis observes, "It is interesting to notice that [Chrétien] places his ideal in the past. For him already 'the age of chivalry is dead.' It always was: let no one think the worse of it on that account." He goes on to explain that "these phantom periods for which the historian searches in vain . . . all have their place in a history

more momentous than that which commonly bears the name."
Lewis seems to suggest that golden ages and ideal places never
were and always are.

Magic

Nowadays the word *magic* refers most often to sleight-of-hand
tricks performed by entertainers. Lewis used the term more
seriously and more broadly to describe anything marvelous or
unexplained, from divine mysteries to diabolical sorcery. Most
of the ideas and attitudes in the chronicles stay consistent from
the first book in the series to the last. But the word *magic* generally takes on darker connotations as the series progresses from
the first books published, *The Lion, the Witch and the Wardrobe*
(1950) and *Prince Caspian* (1951), to later ones such *The Silver
Chair* (1953) and *The Magician's Nephew* (1955).

In general, Lewis thought it was a mistake to associate
magic too closely with the Middle Ages. As he explained in *The
Abolition of Man* (1943), "You will find people who write about
the sixteenth century as if Magic were a medieval survival and
Science the new thing that came to sweep it away. Those who
have studied the period know better. There was very little Magic
in the Middle Ages: the sixteenth and seventeenth centuries are
the high noon of Magic." In *English Literature in the Sixteenth Century, Excluding Drama* (1954), Lewis amplifies on the difference
between medieval magic and that practiced in later centuries.
He explains that the magic found in Arthurian tales is mainly a
literary device, "part of the furniture of romance." In later generations, magic began to be studied as an actual science, an art

for controlling occult forces through incantations, secret formulas, and so on. Merlin works his marvels spontaneously, but later magicians such as Marlowe's Dr. Faustus and Shakespeare's Prospero (in *The Tempest*) must study from arcane books and pronounce dark oaths in order to wield their powers.

Lewis generally considered medieval magic to be "white," paranormal power that could be harnessed by good people. He associated later centuries (what we would call the Renaissance) with *goetia,* the black magic of those who try to make deals with the devil. Yet he never seemed too sure about the boundary between white and black magic, and he suggested it was best to stay away from either kind. In his novel *That Hideous Strength* (1945), Merlin is awakened from an enchanted sleep not only for the service of his secret arts but also so that his own soul may be saved. Even though he is a white magician, he is described as an injured soul, withered from having exposed himself to forces that humans should avoid.

In *The Lion, the Witch and the Wardrobe,* the word *magic* is associated mainly with the mysterious workings of Aslan. After Lucy and Edmund have both visited Narnia on their own, the four Pevensie children all jump into the wardrobe together as if "some magic in the house had come to life and was chasing them into Narnia." (We learn later that everything happens for a purpose in this world, and they have actually been called into Narnia to end the hundred years' winter of the White Witch.) At the end of that book, the word *magic* takes on rich theological dimensions in the Deep Magic of law from the dawn of time and the Deeper Magic of redemption from before time began.

In contexts like this, Lewis sometimes used the word *magical* where most writers would use the word *mystical*. In *Letters to Malcolm* (1964), for example, he described the Christian doctrine of real presence in the elements of Holy Communion as "strong magic." Though the word *magic* usually has negative connotations in Lewis, referring to human attempts to master occult forces, he sometimes resorted to that term when discussing unfathomable mysteries of the Divine.

In the second and third Narnia books published, the word *magic* begins to take on more ambiguous connotations. Caspian's tutor, Doctor Cornelius, calls himself "a very imperfect magician," who knows enough to cast sleeping spells or to find Caspian by means of a crystal. Yet without explaining, Cornelius tells Caspian that the art of practical magic is "not a proper study for princes." Coriakin in *The Voyage of the "Dawn Treader"* is another imperfect magician. His flaw, however, is not in his secret arts but in his soul. We later learn that he once was a star and that his task of ruling the mischievous Monopods is a kind of punishment for some untold moral fault. When Coriakin says he wishes he could rule his subjects by wisdom instead of "rough magic," his words remind us of Prospero in Shakespeare's *The Tempest*. Near the end of the play, Prospero decides to break his sorcerer's staff and "drown" his book of spells. "But this rough magic I here abjure," he proclaims, saying he will live thenceforth only by his natural wits and strength. Lewis commended this act of renunciation, and it may be that Coriakin will not recoup his starring role until he has learned to do the same.

In *The Silver Chair* (1953), originally published fourth in the series, the problem with magic is made even more clear. Jill Pole, who's never been to Narnia, suggests to her friend Eustace that they try to travel to that enchanted world by drawing a circle on the ground and reciting special incantations. Eustace, who is more experienced in the ways of Aslan, pronounces that approach "rather rot," explaining that you can't compel the lordly lion to do your will but can only make a request. This theme is developed more explicitly in *The Magician's Nephew* (1955), the last of the chronicles that Lewis finished writing. Digory's Uncle Andrew is an archetype of the wicked sorcerer. He wants to manipulate occult forces for his own gain, exempts himself from ordinary morality because of his "high and lonely destiny," and disregards the sanctity of life, whether human or animal.

Though he is essentially a comic character, Andrew's magic shares a great deal with the misguided scientism Lewis found all too prevalent in the modern era. In *The Abolition of Man,* for example, Lewis warned that beyond the obvious practical benefits of modern science, there could emerge a kind of religious energy very much like the old occult arts: "There is something which unites magic and applied science while separating both from the 'wisdom' of earlier ages. For the wise men of old the cardinal problem had been how to conform the soul to reality, and the solution had been knowledge, self-discipline, and virtue. For magic and applied science alike the problem is how to subdue reality to the wishes of men." Here Lewis touches on one of the themes that was closest to his heart: learning to accept what is given and to conform one's will to reality, rather than insisting on one's own way and trying to bend reality to one's will. Apart from the intrinsic dangers of the occult, the practice of magic also suggests an underlying attitude of not accepting one's creatureliness, of trying to escape the inevitable vulnerability of being human. Though Aslan's magic is a mystery, it is a benign mystery. But when humans turn to magic, they too often succumb to the old temptation recorded in the book of Genesis: "Ye shall be as gods."

Astrology

Since Lewis often expressed his disapproval of magic, except for divine magic, it might be supposed that he would reject astrology as well. But Lewis explains in *English Literature in the Sixteenth Century* that magic and astrology were never allied. While the first occult science sought power over nature, the second assumed nature's power over humans. Lewis also noted that medieval astrologers did not believe the planets compelled human behavior, only that they influenced it. The usual view in the Middle Ages, he says, was that a person, assisted by grace, could overcome a bad horoscope just as he or she could overcome a naturally bad temper.

In Narnia, astrology is the province of the learned and the wise. In *Prince Caspian,* Doctor Cornelius sees the star named Tarva, Lord of Victory, coming close to Alambil, Lady of Peace. He correctly interprets this to mean that good is coming soon to Narnia. Later in the book, the noble centaur Glenstorm already knows about the War of Deliverance before he is told, because he is "a prophet and a stargazer." In *The Last Battle,* another stargazing centaur, Roonwit, finds an opposite omen, the worst conjunction he has seen in five hundred years. He predicts rightly that great trouble is coming to Narnia and that the supposed Aslan being talked about is a false one.

Lewis never recommended that people check their horoscopes every morning, but he found astrology imaginatively attractive. For one thing, it encourages humility, a sense that the forces of nature often control us more than we control them. More important, the regular movements of the stars provide a powerful confirmation of the cosmic order. In his first stargazing lesson, Caspian asks Cornelius if two stars might come too close, if they might actually collide. The good doctor tells the young prince not to worry, for "the great lords of the upper sky know the steps of their dance too well for that."

This explanation calls to mind the medieval image of the Great Dance. Though we have become accustomed since Newton's time to thinking of the universe as essentially a mechanism, the medieval picture was much more festive. Lewis noted in one of his lectures on medieval cosmologists that their symbol for the *primum mobile,* the outermost sphere of the cosmos, was a young girl dancing and playing a tambourine. He explains that the orderly movements of the heavenly spheres in the medieval picture "are to be conceived not as those of a machine or even an army, but rather as a dance, a festival, a symphony, a ritual, a carnival, or all of these in one."

Of course, a dance is composed of dancers. In *The Discarded Image,* Lewis explained that medieval thinkers attributed life and even intelligence to the stars. In *The Voyage of the "Dawn Treader,"* the children from earth meet Coriakin, a star on probation, and Ramandu, a star at rest. Ramandu explains that once he has regained his youth, he will "once more tread the great dance." Eustace says that where he comes from, stars are only flaming balls of gas. But Ramandu corrects him: "Even in your

world, my son, that is not what a star is, but only what it is made of." In making this distinction, Ramandu is drawing on a medieval teaching that goes back to Aristotle: that a thing's *substance,* its essence, is not the same as its *accidents,* the elements that compose it.

Lewis's depiction of Narnian stars as beings rather than balls of flame adds a reassuring note to the apocalypse described in *The Last Battle.* In the biblical book of Revelation, stars falling from the sky signify the utter and terrible unmaking of the physical world. The darkness of Narnia's final day is described in more comforting terms: "All the stars were falling: Aslan had called them home."

In *The Discarded Image,* Lewis pieces together the medieval world-picture like a great rose window of stained glass, concluding that "few constructions of the human imagination seem to me to have combined splendour, sobriety, and coherence in the same degree." But then Lewis adds that the medieval model of the cosmos had "a serious defect: it was not true."

Having granted that fact, he goes on to examine the way in which any worldview, including modern ones, can be said to be "true." He notes that the medieval model was not "refuted by the telescope," nor overthrown by empirical evidence in general, but rather by a growing awareness of how much more economically the Copernican model explained the movements of stars and planets. Lewis concludes that "no model is a catalogue of ultimate realities, and none is a mere fantasy. Each is a serious attempt to get all the phenomena known at a given period, and each succeeds in getting in a great many. But also, no less surely, each reflects the prevalent psychology of an age almost as much as it reflects the state of that age's knowledge."

As seen in the Narnia stories, Lewis was more drawn to the "prevalent psychology" of the Middle Ages than to that he saw in many of his contemporaries. As a creative writer, he reveled in such a glad, elegant, and orderly picture of the cosmos. As a twentieth-century scholar, he conceded that the medieval picture of the universe was not scientifically accurate. But he found there a wisdom more momentous than that which often goes by the name of science.

CHAPTER SIX

What's in a Narnian Name?

All his life, Lewis had a fascination for names and nicknames. He began by naming himself, of course, deciding at the age of three that he would be called Jack, not Clive. A few years later, he began calling his brother Warren "Badger" or "Badge." In their teen years, the two boys called their father the Pudaita, based on his rounded Irish pronunciation of the word *potato*. (Eventually, this moniker evolved into Pudaitabird.) They also referred to the senior Lewis as His Excellenz, because of his imperious manner, or the Old Air Balloon, because of his bombastic style of speaking. Lewis christened his childhood friend Arthur Greeves "Galahad" because of his idealistic turn of mind. In his teens, Lewis even advised "Galahad" on what to name his new puppy. He warned against commonplace names, saying a dog's name should "suit his character and appearance." He added that if the dog were brisk and warlike, it might be called Sigurd or Mars. If it were quaint and homely, it could go by Bickernocker or Knutt.

Later on in life, when he began publishing fiction, Lewis took the same care that his characters' names should suit their personality and appearance. In *The Screwtape Letters* (1942), he introduces a senior devil, Screwtape, offering advice to his nephew, an apprentice tempter called Wormwood. Some of their infernal colleagues have witty diabolical names such as Toadpipe, Triptweeze, Slumtrimpet, and Slubgob. In *Perelandra* (1943), Lewis imagines Venus as a still unfallen world; its Adam and Eve have the lilting names of Tor and Tinidril. The god figure in *Perelandra,* the second book of the Space Trilogy, is called Maleldil. Though Lewis critics have expended a great deal of ingenuity trying to interpret the meaning of the word, Lewis wrote that he chose the name for the "liquidity" of its sound.

In the Narnia stories, Lewis showcased his talent for naming, creating nearly two hundred characters with names drawn from Greek, Latin, Hebrew, French, Old English, Norse, Celtic—or sometimes just made up. It's a shame Lewis didn't include a fellow named Xerxes, or some other X name, in one of the Narnia books. If he had, he would have used every letter of the alphabet to name something or someone in the chronicles. Apart from meeting the main characters, readers visiting Narnia will also encounter Arsheesh the fisherman, Bricklethumb the dwarf, Camillo the hare, Drinian the sea captain, Edith the bully, Farsight the eagle, Golg the gnome, Hogglestock the hedgehog, Ilgamuth the warrior, Jewel the unicorn, Kidrash the Calormene ruler, Lilygloves the mole, Moonwood the hare, Nikabrik the dwarf, Olvin the Archenland king, Prunaprismia the stepmother of Caspian, various nefarious Queens, Ramandu the retired star, Sallowpad the raven, Thornbut the dwarf, Uvilas the Telmarine lord, Voltinus the faun, Wimbleweather the giant, Yggdrasil the World Ash Tree, and Zardeenah the Calormene goddess of the moon.

Names as Allusions

As to the world in which we meet all these characters, there is an actual place called Narnia. It is best reached not by climbing into a wardrobe but by boarding a northbound bus from Rome. Narnia, now called Narni, is a mountain village in the Italian province of Umbria. Lewis would have encountered the name as a passing reference in Tacitus, Livy, and other Latin authors, and he probably liked the sound of the name. Lewis found a good many of his Narnian names in books he read, both literature and history. As already noted, he found the name Aslan, which means "lion" in Turkish, in Edward William Lane's translation of *The Thousand and One Nights.* That name may also have appealed to him because the word root *as-* means "God" or "gods" in Old Norse—for example, in Asgard, the realm of the Scandinavian gods.

Sometimes Lewis's nonfiction books provide the best clues as to where he found names for his Narnia characters. The London cabby, Frank, in *The Magician's Nephew,* for example, seems an unlikely candidate to become the first king of Narnia. Even the name sounds wrong; it's just too plain and prosaic for someone destined to rule the realm created by Aslan. But in *Studies in Words,* Lewis explains that the word *frank* originally connoted a nobleman, someone of the Frankish race who ruled England after the Norman Conquest. Frankness, in the Middle Ages, suggested the aristocratic ideals of gentleness, courtesy, and honesty. Eventually, the word was narrowed to mean "candor," sometimes brutal candor. But the simple, honest, and brave Frank the cabhorse driver will rehabilitate the word when he and his wife are called to become the first king and queen of the newborn world.

In *The Last Battle,* there is a similar richness of meaning in the name of the Calormene prince Emeth, a word that means "true, faithful" in Hebrew. Lewis discussed the word in *Reflections on the Psalms;* he explains that it refers to "rock-bottom reality," the firmness of the true path, which is a delight to find after one has been lost in muddy fields. His analogy of reaching the true road, *emeth,* after wandering on the wrong path, fits perfectly the destiny of Emeth, finding at last the Truth he has been faithfully seeking all his life.

Lewis was working on his scholarly survey *English Literature in the Sixteenth Century, Excluding Drama* (1954) at the same time he was composing the Narnia chronicles, and sometimes his scholarly work enlivened his creative work. For example, in his literary tome, Lewis mentioned a minor sixteenth-century poet named John Studley, whose word choices were sometimes unintentionally comical. Studley used terms such as "frostyface" and "topsy turvy" in passages meant to be serious, and he described the hellish river Styx as a "puddle glum." Lewis said he couldn't help but smile over the phrase. And he can't help but make his readers smile when he turns it into the name of his morose marsh-wiggle in *The Silver Chair*—Puddleglum.

In *English Literature in the Sixteenth Century,* Lewis also discussed an Anglican cleric named John Jewel whose heart was good but who was too easily drawn into rash controversies and who even advocated violence to suppress enemies of the

Church. In *The Last Battle,* we meet another Jewel, the unicorn who, with his friend King Tirian, attacks and kills the Calormenes who are treating Talking Beasts as slaves. The narrator uses the same word, *rash,* to describe their action and says that even though they were sorely provoked, "much evil" came of their attacking the Calormenes without giving them any warning or challenge first. Despite this ill-considered moment of righteous rage, Lewis generally portrays Jewel as one of the noblest creatures in all the Narnia books. When the unicorn reaches the new, eternal Narnia, he cries out in joy, "I have come home at last! This is my real country! I belong here. This is the land I have been looking for all my life, though I never knew it till now." In these words, Jewel sounds very much like Lewis himself when he vows in *Mere Christianity,* "I must keep alive in myself the desire for my true country, which I shall not find till after death."

Sometimes readers who recognize an allusion in the chronicles have an early clue as to a character's moral qualities. In *Prince Caspian,* when the young prince's nurse is banished, we are not sure at first what to make of his new tutor, the short, stout Cornelius. But he turns out to be the right sort, one who confirms the truth of "nursery tales" about fauns and Talking Beasts. Cornelius dabbles a bit in "white magic" (not the evil kind that so fascinates Andrew Ketterley in *The Magician's Nephew).* And the faithful tutor's name hints that he is on the right side. It calls to mind Cornelius Agrippa, the fifteenth-century Christian scholar who believed one could practice a certain amount of white magic without danger to one's soul.

By contrast, the Queen of Underland in *The Silver Chair* calls herself "The Lady of the Green Kirtle" when traveling overland. Prince Rilian's mother was killed by a green serpent, and he himself became entranced by a woman whose garment was "green as poison." So Eustace and Polly should probably be suspicious of the charming, mysterious lady they meet in the Northern

Wastes, with her "Color Me Sinister" attire. That archaic word *kirtle* is also revealing because it usually refers to a man's tunic. One of the few texts where a lady's gown is called a *kirtle* is the medieval poem *Sir Gawain and the Green Knight,* one version of which was edited by Lewis's friend J.R.R. Tolkien. There the wife of Bercilak, the Green Knight, wears a dress called a *kirtle* when she tries to seduce the noble Gawain. He resists her charms but unwisely accepts a green sash from her that she claims will offer him magical protection from harm. Perhaps if Eustace and Polly had read the same romances Lewis did, they would have known better than to trust a woman with the disquieting title *Lady of the Green Kirtle.*

Many of the allusions in the chronicles are inserted just for fun. Clodsley Shovel sounds like a good name for a master digger, one of the moles in *Prince Caspian.* But it so happens there was a seventeenth-century British naval hero named Sir Cloudesley Shovel. And Caspian's grim stepmother in the same book is named Prunaprismia, probably a variant of the exclamation often repeated in Charles Dickens's *Little Dorritt:* "Prunes and prisms!" The name may seem even more apt when one recalls that Lewis himself thoroughly disliked prunes.

Lewis's allusions in the chronicles are not intrusive, and they may or may not be recognized without detracting from the story line. In *The Silver Chair,* when Eustace and Jill are carried off to a secret meeting of night birds, Lewis names the chapter "A Parliament of Owls." Some readers will recognize this as an echo of the title of Geoffrey Chaucer's poem *The Parliament of Fowls* (1382). But readers who don't recognize the reference will still learn from the birds what happened to Prince Rilian and what must be done to seek him out.

Names from Classical Languages

Lewis learned Greek and Latin at an early age, and a good many names in the chronicles suggest his familiarity with classical languages. The royal galleon of Narnia is called *Splendour Hyaline,* which combines the Latin word for "shining" with the Greek word *hyalinos,* "glassy." Lewis probably recalled the unusual word *hyaline* from Milton's *Paradise Lost,* where the new-made universe is viewed from the "clear Hyaline, the Glassy Sea" of heaven. The other Narnian ship mentioned in the chronicles, the *Dawn Treader,* lands on an island inhabited by invisible, dull-witted creatures called Monopods, who take their name from Greek *mono,* "one," and *pod,* "foot." Lewis did not invent these creatures; monopods are mentioned in *Natural History* by Pliny the Elder (23–79) and in Sir John Mandeville's *Travels* (1371). But Lewis certainly gave them their fullest imaginative embodiment, describing comical bouncy folks with a single leg and a padded, canoe-shaped foot, "living pogo-sticks," as Evan Gibson calls them.

Some of Lewis's classical borrowings are rather obvious, such as the deep underground world of Bism, "deep pit" in Greek, akin to our words *abyss* and *abysmal.* The name of the desert kingdom Calormen suggests Latin *calor,* "heat," as in our word *calorie* (a measure of heat, of course, not weight). Other names may require a bit more research. Chervy is a good name for the stag in *The Horse and His Boy,* because in Latin, *chervus* means "deer." And that dull grammar text in *Prince Caspian* was written by someone called Pulverulentus Siccus, whose Latin name tells us that he and his book are "dry as dust."

Later in the same book, Caspian meets a whole host of fauns—Mentius, Obentius, Nimienus, Dumnus, Voltinus, Girbius, Oscuns, and others. Lewis scholars have dutifully hauled out their Latin dictionaries and tried to guess the meaning of these names. But unless one is a specialist in faunology and can prove they are by nature deceivers (*mentitus*), kissers (*osculare*), and overindulgers (*nimietas*), it may be safest to assume that Lewis simply created Latin-sounding names for these woodland gods from Roman myth.

Names Chosen for Their Sound

Like his faun's names, Lewis seemed to choose Calormene names based on their sound rather than their meaning. Several critics note that *Tash* means "taint or blot" in Scottish, but that seems a rather mild descriptor and an odd source for such a hideous being. Like many other Calormene names—Shasta, Arsheesh, Rabadash, Kidrash—the word *Tash* features a short *a* vowel sound and a *sh* consonant sound. These are two common features of Middle Eastern languages, as can be seen in English words borrowed from that region—*shah, sherbet, hashish,* and *shish kabob.* The Calormene title Tishroc has an authentic Middle Eastern ring, but Lewis probably picked it up, perhaps unconsciously, from a completely different source. In Edith Nesbit's *The Story of the Amulet,* there is a fictional Egyptian ruler called the Nisroch.

When asked about names he created in his Space Trilogy, such as Glund (Jupiter) and Viritrilbia (Mercury), Lewis replied that they weren't connected to any actual language. He explained, "I am always playing with syllables and fitting them together (purely by ear) to see if I can hatch up new words that please me. I want them to have an emotional, not intellectual, suggestiveness." In a similar vein, Lewis wrote to a child named Joan that he was "in love with syllables." He noted how much he enjoyed names in Tolkien's stories such as Tinuviel and Silmaril. He added that he thought the name Northumberland glorious and wished the phrase *silver salver* meant something interesting, since it had such a lovely sound.

Lewis admitted to having old-fashioned tastes in poetry, and his preferences in sounds reflect traditional poetics. The consonants *l* and *r* (called *liquids*) and *m* and *n* (called *nasals*) are usually considered the most musical, soft-sounding tones. In all of Lewis's books, characters and places associated with the good are dominated by these more melodious consonants: Maleldil, Aslan, Ramandu. Other consonants, such as *f, v,* and *z* (called *fricatives*) and *p, b, j, k, t,* and *d* (called *plosives*) are considered more prosaic and harsh-sounding. Lewis's bad characters tend to have dissonant-sounding names that contain these harsher consonants. The devils in *The Screwtape Letters,* with names like Toadpipe and Slubgob, illustrate the point. But so do negative characters in the chronicles, with names such as Gumpas, Nikabrik, and Edith Jackle.

Kings of Narnia generally have "liquid" names—Rilian, Erlian, Tirian. So when someone comes along called Jadis or

Miraz and claims to be the rightful ruler of Narnia, the very sound of the name should arouse suspicion. Caspian is a good Narnian king with a bad lineage (Telmarine pirates), and the sound of his name, poetically speaking, begins badly but ends well.

One of the names Lewis had suggested as a teenager for a dog that was "quaint and homely" was Knutt, a word with a short *u* vowel sound. When Lewis wrote the chronicles thirty years later, he continued to favor names with short *u* vowels for his quaint and homely characters. Besides Trumpkin the dwarf and Tumnus the faun, there are Trufflehunter the badger, the comical Dufflepuds, and Rumblebuffin the giant. Setting the record with four short *u*'s in his name is the obsequious gnome Mullugutherum in *The Silver Chair*.

Other characters in the chronicles are named after the sounds they make. Reepicheep and Peepicheek have names, of course, which call to mind the squeaky voices of mice. The two Talking Horses, Bree and Hwin, also have names based on the sounds they make. Bree explains to Shasta that his full name is "Breehy-hinny-brinny-hoohy-hah," something like the sound of a whinny. Hwin's name is also based on the word whinny. Like many words now beginning with *wh-*, this word was spelled in Old English (and is still properly pronounced) *hw-*.

Names of Other Talking Beasts

Though Bree and Hwin are the two most prominent equine characters in the chronicles, horses and centaurs figure prominently in several other Narnia books, and many of these have memorable names. Some names are self-explanatory, such as

Snowflake, the Queen of Underland's white horse, and Coal-black, Rilian's dark horse, in *The Silver Chair*. The London cabby's horse Strawberry in *The Magician's Nephew* is probably also named after his appearance, as that is a common name for horses whose mix of chestnut and white hairs give them a pinkish tone. When Aslan turns Strawberry into a winged horse, he renames him Fledge, which means "to grow feathers needed for flying." (A *fledgling* is a young bird just getting its feathers; *full-fledged* literally means "fully feathered.") The horses mentioned in *Prince Caspian* have French names. Caspian's horse Destrier takes his name from the Old French word for "warhorse." Lord Glozelle's horse, Pomely, means "dappled."

Though centaurs come from classical mythology, Narnian centaurs have solid English names: Glenstorm, Cloudbirth, and Roonwit. These compound creatures—half man, half horse—have compound names, imitating Anglo-Saxon *kennings* (poetic paraphrases, such as "whale-road" as a name for the sea). The most famous centaur in classical mythology was Chiron, who taught music, medicine, and hunting to Achilles, Hercules, and other fabled heroes. Lewis seems to model his centaurs after Chiron, as they are noble creatures of wisdom, strength, and learning. Glenstorm is a prophet and stargazer in *Prince Caspian* who aids the young prince in regaining his rightful throne. The meaning of the centaur's name becomes clear the first time he appears in the story. As Caspian and his companions enter a "great glen or wooded gorge," they call the centaur's name; suddenly, they hear the sound of hoofs, which grows louder, until the valley trembles. There, amid trampled thickets, they see Glenstorm and his three sons, great warriors who came storming down the glen when they were called by their king. Cloudbirth, whose name suggests almost celestial origins, is a renowned healer who is called to help mend Puddleglum's burnt foot at the end of *The Silver Chair*. And Roonwit, in *The Last Battle,* has the "wit" to read "roons." That is, he is knowledgeable in mysteries and ancient letters (runes). Like Glenstorm, Roonwit can read the stars; he is the one who sees great trouble in the skies and who suspects that the imperious new Aslan who has appeared recently in Narnia is a false one.

While Reepicheep the mouse and Hwin the horse are named for the way they sound, other Talking Beasts in Narnia are named for the way they look or the way they act. Glimfeather is a great white owl whose feathers glimmer in the moonlight. Lilygloves the mole is never described, but it may be safely guessed that this prodigious digger has white forepaws. Similarly, the raven's name Sallowpad means "pale-footed." Ginger, the conniving tomcat in *The Last Battle,* is also named for his coloring—orangy-brown like the spice. (Lewis owned a tomcat named Ginger at the time he was writing the chronicles.)

Another furtive furball in *The Last Battle* is Slinkey the fox, an ally of the Calormenes, who presumably slinks around betraying his fellow Narnians. The name of Pattertwig the squirrel in *Prince Caspian* suggests both his pattering feet along the branches of trees and his chattering tongue. Trufflehunter, the badger in the same book, is someone who would like to go looking for truffles, the underground tubers he regards as a delicacy. Badgers are known for their powerful jaws, so it makes sense that their clan in Narnia is called the Hardbiters. Trufflehunter explains his own steadfastness as part of his nature: "I'm a beast and we don't change. I'm a badger, what's more, and we hold on."

Names of Evil Beings

When the White Witch prepares to slay Aslan in *The Lion, the Witch and the Wardrobe,* she gathers about her a regular parliament of foul creatures, including ghouls, ogres, and wolves as well as "Cruels and Hags and Incubuses, Wraiths, Horrors, Efreets, Sprites, Orknies, Wooses, and Ettins." This menacing menagerie includes evil beings from classical, Germanic, Celtic, and Islamic mythologies. Cruels and Horrors are cruel and horrible, of course. Lewis sometimes enjoyed playing with words, turning modifiers into nouns. In *The Great Divorce,* for example, he describes a lady who had been grumbling so long that she just turned into a grumble.

A hag is not just an ugly old woman but an actual witch. The name is a shortened form of "hedge rider," from the old belief that witches rode their brooms along hedgerows at night. An incubus is also a spirit of the night, a demon who lies down on people as they sleep. (Oddly, the same Latin root provides the word *incubate,* which originally meant "to lie on an egg until it hatches.") *Sprite* is a variant of *spirit*; obviously, in this context, not effervescent, but evil.

Since Horrors bring on horror, some readers of *The Lion, the Witch and the Wardrobe* assume that Wooses make people woozy. But *wooses* is most likely a variant form of the archaic term *woses,* wild people of the woods. Orknies are monsters mentioned in the Anglo-Saxon saga *Beowulf,* spelled *orcneas* in Old English. (Tolkien's orcs are derived from the same source.) Also from Anglo-Saxon is *ettin,* an archaic name for an evil giant. This word appears again in *The Silver Chair,* where Eustace, Jill, and Puddleglum are forced to cross the Ettinsmoor, the plain of giants. *Wraith* is a Celtic word, the name for a phantom or apparition. (This term also appears in *The Lord of the Rings,* in which the Ringwraiths have become spectral slaves of Sauron.) The Efreets who join the White Witch come all the way from the Middle East. Efreets are ghouls or evil jinn (genies) of Islamic legend. The White Witch herself is an evil jinn who is associated with Lilith from Hebrew lore; she is apparently a malicious amalgam of Jewish and Islamic mythologies.

The White Witch seems also to be a new embodiment of Jadis, the evil queen in *The Magician's Nephew.* Lewis explained in *Studies in Words* that the word *villain* was from French and originally referred to a peasant villager, someone not at all *frank.* And in the chronicles, many of Lewis's villains take their names from French. As noted in the preceding chapter, Jadis comes from the French word for "times of yore," perhaps a reference to the dead world of Charn, which she has destroyed. Charn is also from French, suggesting a graveyard. (The phrase *charnel house,* a depository of bodies or bones, is from the same source.) The White Witch's chief of police is called Maugrim in the original English editions, a name that combines Old French *maugre,* "ill will," with *grim.* In *Prince Caspian,* there is a new usurper to be defeated; his name, Miraz, suggests *mirage,* a false appearance. And this false king's treacherous aide is named Glozelle, French for "flatterer, deceiver."

Names of the Children

Early in 1949, C. S. Lewis's friend and fellow author Sister Penelope said she was thinking of adopting a pen name for one of her books and asked if he had any suggestions. Lewis replied with several names for her to consider, one of which was Pevensey. He didn't give any reason for the name; he probably just liked the sound of it. Sister Penelope never used the *nom de plume,* but it didn't go to waste. When *The Lion, the Witch and the Wardrobe* was published the following year, the four children who first entered Narnia were the Pevensies. Apparently, Lewis had found a name he liked before he created the characters to go with it.

As for their given names, Lewis seemed to choose what he considered common English names most young readers would find familiar. In his early draft, the four evacuees were called Ann, Martin, Rose, and Peter, the last one being the youngest. When Lewis returned to the project nearly ten years later, the names became Peter, Susan, Edmund, and Lucy, with Peter now the oldest. The one passage where Peter's name takes on added significance is in *The Last Battle,* when Aslan commands Peter, as High King, to shut the door on the dark, cold space that had once been the old Narnia. Peter pulls the door closed and locks it with a golden key, a gesture that calls to mind the scene in the Gospels in which Jesus tells his disciple Peter he will give him the keys to the Kingdom of Heaven.

Lewis dedicated the first Narnia story to be published, *The Lion, the Witch and the Wardrobe,* to his godchild Lucy Barfield, the daughter of his lifelong friend Owen Barfield. Surely, it is no accident that the most pure-hearted character in the chronicles is also named Lucy. Eustace's co-adventurer Jill in *The Silver Chair* may also be named in honor of someone Lewis knew. One of the evacuees who came to the Kilns during World War II was Jill Flewett, who lived there for two years and won the hearts of everyone in the household. The Lewis brothers stayed in touch with Jill after she left Oxford and took up an acting career. One of the very few films they attended was *The Woman in the Hall* (1947), in which she appeared under the name Jill Raymond. It may be only a coincidence, but when Jill and Eustace first arrive in Narnia, Glimfeather the owl confronts them and asks, in his hooting speech, "But who are you? There's something magic about you two. I saw you arrive: you *flew*." The word *flew* is italicized in the text, perhaps a typographical tribute to the young lady Lewis admired so much, Jill Flewett.

Of course, Eustace's name stands out from among the other, more common children's names. This is intentional, as Lewis makes clear in the opening sentence of *The Voyage of the "Dawn Treader"*: "There was a boy called Eustace Clarence Scrubb, and he almost deserved it." That line has made several critics wonder about a boy called Clive Staples Lewis, who felt he didn't deserve it. (The other character in the series who most resembles Lewis has the funny name of Digory.) Eustace is portrayed as a cad and a snob in the early chapters of *Voyage,* and Lewis admitted to being something of "a fop, a cad, and a snob" during his time away at boarding school. Though he was never a utilitarian fact-monger like Eustace, the young Lewis did write home to Ireland about being surrounded by "coarse, brainless English schoolboys" at Malvern College.

There also seems to be a bit of the author in Eustace's "undragoning" episode later in *The Voyage of the "Dawn Treader."* Eustace wanders away from the others and falls asleep on a dragon's horde, thinking greedy, dragonish thoughts. Turned into a dragon himself by some unknown spell, he realizes he has become "a monster cut off from the whole human race" and admits to himself that he has been a self-centered brat the whole voyage. Though the narrator explains that everyone noticed that

"Eustace's character had been rather improved by becoming a dragon," he is eager to resume his human form but doesn't know how. Then one night, Aslan appears to him by moonlight, as in a dream, and carries him off to a place with fruit trees and a wide well like a great marble bath. Eustace tries to scratch off his dragon scales, only to find yet another layer of scales underneath, and then another. Finally, he agrees to let Aslan take over, and the great lion seems to rip his dragon flesh to the very core of his being. Then Aslan picks him up and tosses him into the water, which stings at first but then feels delightful. Through great fear and pain, Eustace is given back his human form. The story goes on to explain that though he still had his bad days, Eustace from that time on "began to be a different boy" because "the cure had begun."

Eustace's undragoning is a kind of symbolic baptism, an experience of self-transformation that he could not have accomplished on his own. He comes to see that the secret of change lies in submission, not self-effort. This is a lesson very similar to one found in Lewis's letters during his period of spiritual transition in his early thirties. About six months after his turn toward theism, Lewis wrote his friend Arthur that things were going well for him spiritually, yet he had to admit to being something of a "conceited ass" (the same term used to describe Eustace in

The Voyage of the "Dawn Treader"). Lewis told Arthur he was still struggling, especially with pride and willfulness: "There seems to be no end to it. Depth under depth of self-love and self-admiration. Closely connected with this is the difficulty I find in making even the faintest approach to giving up my own will." A few years later, Lewis would write that all such regimens of self-effort were ultimately futile. In *The Pilgrim's Regress,* the first book he wrote after his conversion to Christianity, Lewis quoted Augustine's advice that you must "throw yourself down safely"— that is, let go and trust yourself to Another.

When Eustace returns in *The Silver Chair,* the narrator introduces him by saying, "His name unfortunately was Eustace Scrubb, but he wasn't a bad sort." The priggish name hasn't changed, but the little boy has. Thinking of his own spiritual journey, the writer may have felt the same way about Clive Staples Lewis.

CHAPTER SEVEN

Lewis's Literary Artistry

Ever since they were first published, the Narnia stories have been enthusiastically received by the reading public. The chronicles have gone through scores of printings in England and America, and continue to sell well over a million copies a year. (In some years, half of all new sales have been among college students.) From the mid-1950s onward, Lewis received stacks of cards and letters every day, many from children. He tried to answer as many of these letters as he could, occasionally jotting little drawings in the margin. Some of Lewis's most winsome replies to the thousands of letters he received have been collected in his *Letters to Children*, an eloquent testimony to how seriously he took his readers of all ages.

Despite the ongoing success of the Narnia chronicles, some may be surprised to see the words *literary artistry* applied to children's literature. After all, aren't these stories meant as a diversion, something for reading to little ones to help them fall asleep? Lewis the critic defended this kind of story as serious literary expression, and Lewis the creative writer illustrated just how artful this genre can be.

Lewis was greatly influenced by the now-classic defense of fantasy literature, "On Fairy-Stories," composed by his friend J.R.R. Tolkien. This essay argues that the unique domain of fairy stories is the realm of Faerie, the perilous realm of magic and enchantment where ordinary mortals must sometimes venture to fulfill a quest. For Tolkien, an authentic fairy story is not simply an extension of our primary world but the creation of a plausible and self-consistent secondary world that is subject to its own laws. Fantasy, for Tolkien, is at heart the "making or glimpsing of Other-worlds."

The notion that an artist is a creator of alternate realities is not a new one. But Tolkien's strategy is to suggest that this exalted model of artistic creation is best embodied not in the novel or epic but in that humble genre, the fairy story. Just as Tolkien argued in another famous essay that *Beowulf* should be considered as literature, not as a historical artifact, here he argues that fairy stories should be esteemed as literature, not as pastimes for children. When critic Edmund Wilson characterized Tolkien's epic, *The Lord of the Rings*, as "a children's book which has somehow got out of hand," he was voicing the very prejudice that Tolkien sought to overcome in "On Fairy-Stories."

The doctrine of subcreation was especially congenial to Tolkien, both as a Christian and as a fantasy writer. As a Christian, Tolkien could view subcreation as a form of worship, a way for creatures to express the divine image in them by becoming creators. As a fantasy writer, Tolkien could affirm his chosen genre as one of the purest of all fictional modes because it called for the creation not only of characters and incidents but also of worlds for them to inhabit.

C. S. Lewis endorsed Tolkien's theory of subcreation, and he recommended "On Fairy-Stories" to those who asked him about his own views on fantasy. Yet his own essay on the subject, "Sometimes Fairy Stories May Say Best What's to Be Said," strikes a rather different note. This brief but illuminating essay begins by distinguishing two sides of the writer: the author and the person. The author writes simply to release a creative impulse, an idea or a compelling image "longing for a form," for some coherent expression. Soon, however, the person enters into the writing process with his or her own values and purposes, a desire to shape the writing toward some significant end. The author may write only to please—oneself or one's readers—but the person wishes to both please and instruct, to communicate some of one's own views of the world.

This dual emphasis is only a slight variation on Tolkien's essay, but it helps explain the markedly different character of the two men's work—as well as Tolkien's remark that the Narnia stories were "outside the range of [his] sympathy." Though Tolkien expressed his values implicitly in *The Lord of the Rings,* he affirmed the author's act of subcreation as an end in itself. Lewis agreed that a writer can't even begin without the author's urge to create but felt he shouldn't begin without a desire to communicate his sense of the world and our place in it.

Tolkien's and Lewis's differing views of fantasy literature are evident not only in their critical essays but also in their creative works. Tolkien was committed to the *independence* of his created secondary world from our primary world. In the fifteen hundred pages of *The Lord of the Rings,* Tolkien studiously avoids any literary or historical references that would draw readers' attention away from his fictive world and make them think of our own. Tolkien objected to the Narnia chronicles because Lewis unabashedly introduces in his secondary world characters and motifs taken from our primary world—classical deities, biblical images, historical allusions, and even references to trains, radios, and cars.

Obviously, Lewis did not view these references as an artistic lapse, as the failure of a subcreator to create an independent world. Rather, he delighted in stressing the *interdependence* of his created secondary worlds and our primary world. This emphasis on the interpenetration of our real world with the fictive world of Narnia allowed Lewis to write fantasy with Christian overtones without feeling that he had undermined the integrity of his art. Despite their difference of emphasis, Tolkien and Lewis wholeheartedly agreed that fantasy literature is a legitimate literary genre all its own, not just something for children. Lewis summed up their shared view: "I am almost inclined to set it up as a canon that a children's story which is enjoyed only by children is a bad children's story."

The Narrator as Character

Lewis's emphasis on the interconnections between his fictional world and our "factual" world was not just a storytelling device; it was a reflection of his own mindscape. In *Surprised by Joy,* Lewis reports that he lived almost entirely in his imagination from the ages of six to eight. He later comments about his school days: "My secret, imaginative life began to be so important and so distinct from my outer life that I almost have to tell two stories." Even as an adult, there was an "outer Lewis" who gave lectures, met with friends, and took care of his domestic responsibilities. But there was an equally real "inner Lewis" whose mental vision was focused on other times and places, other worlds of imagination, and unseen realities affirmed by faith.

In his fiction, Lewis put this two-sidedness to good use. His narrator in the Space Trilogy is named Lewis, a university don like himself, except that he has conversed with angels and has a friend, Elwin Ransom, who has traveled to Mars and Venus. Lewis's alter ego, the Lewis of the trilogy, sounds so convincing that letters came to the Kilns from readers asking if all this really happened. With amusement, Lewis exclaimed, "Some people just don't understand what fiction is."

In the chronicles, the narrator again reminds us of Lewis himself. This fictive voice is a vivid personality in his own right; he sounds like a kindly, keen-eyed uncle telling stories by the fireside or the bedside. This narrator as storyteller is one of Lewis's most impressive achievements in the Narnia series. Critic Peter J. Schakel has ably argued that after Aslan himself, the narrator is the most important character in the chronicles, the one who provides artistic cohesion for diverse ensembles of characters, settings, and plotlines.

The narrator of the chronicles matter-of-factly assumes that the world of Narnia and our world are interconnected. In *The Lion, the Witch and the Wardrobe,* he says that a giant with a happy, beaming face is a sight well worth seeing, since "giants of any sort are now so rare in England." In *The Silver Chair,* he tells the reader, if you ever find your way to Narnia, be sure to visit the cave where Rilian and his rescuers emerged from Under-land. And in *The Voyage of the "Dawn Treader,"* he explains that the music one hears near the World's End would break your heart, yet it is not at all sad—something he learned by talking to Lucy Pevensie herself.

As these examples show, the narrator of the Narnia tales speaks in a conversational tone, often referring to himself as *I.* In *The Magician's Nephew,* he explains that Digory wondered what Polly was doing but adds, "You need not wonder, for I am going to tell you." In *The Lion, the Witch and the Wardrobe,* he remarks that all the Pevensie children thought newly cooked freshwater fish was delicious and interjects, "And I agree with them." He also mentions the legend that King Arthur will someday return to Britain and adds, "And I say the sooner the better."

The narrator also frequently refers to the reader as *you,* someone he seems to know personally. When the Pevensie chil-dren come to the beach near Cair Paravel, the narrator describes the seaweed, the salt air, and the endless blue-green waves and then asks, "And, oh, the cry of the seagulls! Have you heard it? Do you remember?" In *The Horse and His Boy,* he says that Shasta had never experienced the delightful smell of frying bacon, eggs, and mushrooms before but adds, "I hope you have." In *The Silver Chair,* he spends a whole paragraph speaking directly to readers, trying to help them visualize Jill's dizzying vista when looking down from the unimaginable heights of Aslan's country.

In the final page of *The Last Battle,* the narrator identifies directly with his readers: "And for us this is the end of all the stories, and we can most truly say that they all lived happily ever after. But for them it was only the beginning of the real story."

In this closing, Lewis the narrator and Lewis the fiction writer and person of faith come together. In his imagined otherworld, the greatest stories are just beginning. But both the writer and the reader have come to the end of the last page and must now return to the outer world of the here and now. By that time, many readers will have developed as much affection for the story-teller of the chronicles as they have for some of their favorite characters such as Reepicheep or Puddleglum.

Are the Chronicles Politically Incorrect?

Since the narrating voice of the chronicles sounds so much like Lewis himself, it is reasonable ask how much the stories reflect his own values and social attitudes. Though the Narnia stories have generally been quite well received by the public and by pundits, there have also been debunkers and detractors. The most common criticisms focus on violence in the chronicles or on attitudes that seem sexist and racist.

The question of violence in children's stories predates the chronicles by at least a century. About the same time that *folk tales,* intended for everyone, were redefined as *fairy tales,* stories for children, the question suddenly arose about whether the old tales were too grisly. In earlier versions, Goldilocks gets eaten by the bears and Red Cap (Little Red Riding Hood) suffers a similar fate at the paws of her surprisingly toothy granny. Such episodes do not necessarily make for sweet dreams, so most of the traditional tales were supplied with less disturbing endings in the nineteenth century. G. K. Chesterton was one of the first to argue that fairy tales do not create fears in children but actually give them a way to cope with their fears:

> Fairy tales are not responsible for producing fear in children. . . . Fairy tales do not give the child the idea of the evil or the ugly; that is in the child already, because it is in the world already. Fairy tales do not give a child his first idea of a bogey. What fairy tales give the child is his first clear idea that a bogey may be defeated. The baby has known the dragon intimately ever since he had an imagination. What the fairy tale provides for him is a St. George to kill the dragon.

Lewis's own view on violence in children's literature echoes that of Chesterton, one of his favorite authors. As someone who suffered nightmares all his life, Lewis said he did not underrate the concern that fantasy stories might increase children's fears. But he contrasted phobias and nightmares with the feigned excitement induced by reading about adventure-story dangers from goblins or robbers. He found it odd that children who knew about secret police and atom bombs in the real world should be asked to avoid stories with evil forces or battle scenes. Like Chesterton, he believed children learn early on that we live in a world of "death, violence, wounds, adventure, heroism and cowardice, good and evil." Rather than shield children from the darker side of life, he thought it best to show them that light can overcome darkness, that heroic action can defeat evil.

Lewis was genuinely concerned about any bad effects his stories might have on children. He was especially worried that his chapter "The Dark Island" in *The Voyage of the "Dawn Treader"*

might recall too vividly children's own nightmares; he sometimes asked children if they found that episode too frightening.
Even though none of them did, he revised the original English
editions of that chapter when the first American editions came
out, making it clear he sympathized with children who suffer
from night fears. (Unfortunately, in returning to the English
originals, the post-1994 editions of *The Voyage of the "Dawn Treader"*
have omitted Lewis's revisions.)

The chronicles portray characters killed in battle, children
captured and treated as slaves, and a sorceress-serpent hacked
to pieces. Parents know their own children best and may decide
at what age such scenes would not be disturbing. Of course,
most young people these days have witnessed hundreds of sim-
ulated deaths on television, film screens, or video games. So
printed pages in which honorable and good characters always
defeat treachery and evil may not be the primary area of concern for uneasy parents.

Perhaps the most problematic violence in the chronicles is
that which originates with Aslan himself. In *The Horse and His Boy,*
the Calormene princess Aravis receives whiplike scratches on the
back from Aslan, "tear for tear, throb for throb, blood for blood,"
in exchange for the whipping her stepmother's slave received.
Aravis drugged her innocent serving girl in order to escape, and
Aslan wants Aravis to feel empathy for the pain she caused. But
it seems a bit arbitrary for him to invoke in this one instance the
principle of *lex talionis,* the law of retaliation. Lewis makes his
point much more effectively with Edmund in *The Lion, the Witch
and the Wardrobe* or Eustace in *The Voyage of the "Dawn Treader";* in
those cases, it is clear the boys' suffering is the consequence of
their own bad behavior, not punishment meted out by Aslan.

Similarly, at the end of *The Silver Chair,* Aslan himself briefly visits earth to help punish "the Gang" at Experiment House. Though they are more frightened than actually harmed, it seems odd that Aslan would go to such trouble just to give some playground bullies their just deserts. Lewis had an ongoing, unhealed grievance about the way he was treated at boarding school, as seen in his detailed discussion of the subject in *Surprised by Joy* and his caustic satire in *The Silver Chair.* If Lewis's worldview is correct, such bullies will get their due eventually without the need for leonine intervention from another world. Lewis once criticized George MacDonald for occasionally venting "a repressed fund of indignation," using his fiction to "deliver stunning blows" against his adversaries in a way he would never have done in real life. Perhaps Lewis recognized this fault in MacDonald because it was a temptation he sometimes faced in his own writing.

Apart from violence, some reviewers have also complained about sexist attitudes in the chronicles. In a book chapter called "Masking the Misogynist in Narnia," Kath Filmer notes all the

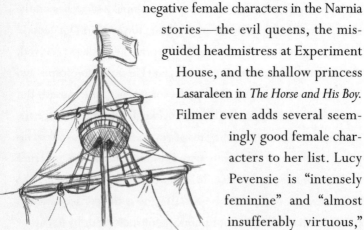

negative female characters in the Narnia stories—the evil queens, the misguided headmistress at Experiment House, and the shallow princess Lasaraleen in *The Horse and His Boy.* Filmer even adds several seemingly good female characters to her list. Lucy Pevensie is "intensely feminine" and "almost insufferably virtuous," while the kindly Mrs. Beaver "fusses and bullies" her husband. For some reason, Filmer fails to mention all the male malefactors in Narnia, including the cowardly Uncle Andrew, the usurping Miraz, the treacherous Sopespian, the murderous Glozelle, the officious Gumpas, the slave-trading Pug, and the shiftless Shift the Ape. In fact, if the "C" in C. S. Lewis stood for Claire instead of Clive, some male critic might wonder why it is always the little boys from earth—Digory, Edmund, Eustace—who cause so much trouble in Narnia or why the narrator tells the story much more often from the point of view of female characters than males.

Lewis grew up in the male-dominated world of English boarding schools and men's colleges at Oxford. And there are slighting references to women, sometimes probably unconscious, in his books and letters. In *Surprised by Joy,* for example, Lewis declares his friend Owen Barfield to be "as fascinating (and infuriating) as a woman," implying that all women share certain generic traits.

In *Mere Christianity,* Lewis affirmed the apostle Paul's views about male headship in the Church and in marriage. But this is not evidence of pathological misogyny, hatred of women, as some critics have suggested. Rather it was orthodox teaching in the Anglican Church of that era. Perhaps it would have been wiser for an unmarried person to speak more tentatively on the topic of gender roles in marriage. When Lewis wed Joy Davidman in 1956, the same year the last of the Narnia chronicles was published, he married a very strong personality and did not seem to invoke his spousal headship very often, if at all.

Despite the views implied in his books, Lewis was universally liked and respected by the women who knew him personally. In published personal reminiscences about Lewis, the female contributors unfailingly describe him in positive terms, while the men offer mixed responses. Patricia (Boshell) Heidelberger, who stayed at the Kilns during the early years of World War II, recalls that Lewis voluntarily coached her in Latin and Greek in order to prepare her for studies at Oxford and that he made a secret arrangement with her mother to pay her tuition. Jill Flewett, who also stayed at the Kilns during the war, remembers that Lewis lent her books and even allowed her to charge books on his account at Blackwell's. She says that Lewis built up her self-esteem and taught her to believe in herself as an intelligent human being. Lewis also paid for her to have professional acting lessons. Rosamund Cowan, one of Lewis's first female pupils, said she was intimidated at first because of his reputation as a "man's man," but she found him courteous, stimulating, intellectually demanding—in sum, "a joy to study with." Though Lewis's books sometimes contain remarks about women that one might expect from an Oxford bachelor, his attitude in person manifested itself primarily in the form of sensitivity, courtesy, generosity, and respect.

In the chronicles, it is usually the villains who make sexist remarks. Uncle Andrew in *The Magician's Nephew* dismisses traditional ethics as "old wives' tales" and says Digory has too many scruples because he was "brought up among women." In *The Lion, the Witch and the Wardrobe,* Edmund says it's "just like a girl" for Lucy to go off and sulk. In *Prince Caspian,* Miraz dismisses the "womanish councils" of his advisers. And the evil prince Rabadash in *The Horse and His Boy* explains Susan's rejection of him by saying, "For it is well known that women are as changeable as weathercocks." In general, negative male characters in the Narnia stories are most easily identified by their patronizing attitudes toward others, especially females.

For some critics, the main problem with the chronicles is not sexism but racism. Andrew Blake, for example, objects to Lewis's Calormenes as an unkind parody of Arabs, concluding that the Narnia books contribute to the contemporary "demonization of Islam." On this last point, Blake is surely mistaken. Islam is strictly monotheistic, its foundational teaching that there is no god but God (Allah). The Calormenes, by contrast, speak of their "gods," including Tash, Azaroth, and Zardeenah. Also, in the Islamic tradition, Allah speaks through his prophets. He does not physically come to earth as Tash does. In fact, Tash is much more similar to an Efreet, an evil spirit of hideous appearance and foul odor, as described in *The Thousand and One Nights*. In the figure of Tash, Lewis is not demonizing Islam; he is demonizing demons, as depicted in Middle Eastern folklore.

The Calormenes resemble Arabs in many respects because Lewis, by his own account, modeled them after characters in *The Arabian Nights*. Every objectionable trait associated with the Calormenes can easily be found in Lewis's source materials, which arose among Middle Easterners themselves, not among biased outsiders. Even so, it was probably unwise for Lewis to generalize about a whole people, even a fictional people. Europeans would not want to be judged according to Grimm's fairy tales, stories where witches, wolves, and woodsmen do not provide a full or balanced picture of medieval society in Europe.

In the chronicles, Lewis made it a point to condemn racism. When Nikabrik, the mean-spirited dwarf in *Prince Caspian,* calls Dr. Cornelius a "renegade dwarf" and a "half-and-halfer," the sensible Trumpkin tells him to be quiet, as a "creature can't help its ancestry." Throughout the chronicles, Aslan interacts with characters one on one, not as types or social groups. Among the Calormenes, the two characters we get to know best are Aravis and Emeth, individuals whom readers are invited to like and admire. And when Lucy arrives in the new, eternal Narnia, she sees the great city of Tashbaan there too. Apparently, Emeth is only one of many Calormenes who has always been serving Aslan, in spirit if not in name.

Lewis as Critic and Lewis as Creator

Though the chronicles have attracted some criticisms that deserve consideration, it would be highly misleading to treat the Narnia series as controversial or problematic. The overwhelming consensus for nearly half a century has been that the chronicles may well be the crowning achievement in what was already a highly distinguished writing career.

When the Narnia stories were first published, they received generally enthusiastic reviews. Of *The Lion, the Witch and the Wardrobe* (1950), *The Guardian* proclaimed that the story combined "Hans Christian Andersen's power to move and George MacDonald's power to create strange new worlds," adding that the book was "naturally, beautifully written." *Prince Caspian* (1951) was praised in the *Saturday Review* for its "good plot, convincing characters, and the graceful working that distinguishes this writer." *The Voyage of the "Dawn Treader"* (1952) was called a "modern fairy tale classic" in *The New York Times Book Review.* Later books received similar accolades in major journals for their "deft characters, colorful descriptions, and playful bits of satire," their "beautiful writing" and "imaginative power." Once the whole series had been published, the well-known critic Edmund Fuller pronounced them, in the *Chicago Sunday Tribune,* to be "the finest group of stories for children, Christian in theme, written in our times."

Sometimes Lewis the critic, commenting on specific authors and genres, offers unexpected insights about his own creative writing. For example, he praised the novels of Jane Austen for their "undeceptions," moments in which a character who has failed to understand a situation suddenly recognizes the true state of affairs. Lewis included several such undeceptions in the Narnia tales. In *The Silver Chair,* the cold, weary travelers, eager to reach Harfang, take little notice of the odd-shaped structures they see around them in the blizzard or the mazelike trenches they have to cross. Later, they realize they missed two of Aslan's Signs, walking right through the Ruined City and failing to recognize the trenches as the letters UNDER ME carved in stone. Similarly, in *The Voyage of the "Dawn Treader,"* Eustace tries to figure out what is going on in the dragon's cave. He sees two puffs of smoke in front of him and notices a dragon's claw, first on his right, then on his left. He fears he's sitting right next to a dragon. Then, worse yet, he fears he's sitting between *two* dragons. Then, worst of all, comes the undeception: he himself has become a dragon!

Lewis seemed to have a deeper sort of undeception in mind for readers of the chronicles. In his sermon "The Weight of Glory," he explains that we all have within us a "desire for our own far-off country," an "inconsolable secret" that we clumsily label nostalgia or romanticism or our lost youth. If we try to locate this longing for paradise in our own idealized past or the idealized future of social reformers, we are sure to be disappointed. All images of beauty or perfect contentment are only "the scent of a flower we have not found, the echo of a tune we have not heard, news from a country we have never yet visited." Having evoked a certain nameless ache we all feel, Lewis continues: "Do you think I am trying to weave a spell? Perhaps I am; but remember your fairy tales. Spells are used for breaking enchantments as well as for inducing them. And you and I have need of the strongest spell that can be found to wake us from the evil enchantment of worldliness."

Lewis further revealed his own method, and the secret of his artistic achievement, in an essay called "On Three Ways of Writing for Children." There, he comments that fantasy stories are not simply about readers identifying with characters in the book. After all, a child today does not really desire to fend off dragons in his or her own neighborhood. Rather, stories of fairyland arouse "a longing for he knows not what. It stirs and troubles him (to his life-long enrichment) with the dim sense of something beyond his reach and, far from dulling or emptying the actual world, gives it a new dimension of depth. He does not despise real woods because he has read of enchanted woods: the reading makes all real woods a little enchanted."

For Lewis, too many things about our contemporary world have become dreary and unenchanted. By inviting readers to a place called Narnia, he wants to re-enchant us, to revive our sense of wonder, to regale our inner vision with adventures of great peril and greater promise. He seeks as well to renew our hope, to suggest a bright benevolence at the heart of things—not only in imagined worlds but also in our own.

APPENDIX

Definitions, Allusions, and Textual Notes

Lewis stated that his use of the fairy-tale form in the Narnia chronicles imposed "severe limitations on vocabulary" (*Of Other Worlds,* 37), presumably so that young readers would have no difficulty with his prose. But again, it seems that Lewis was writing for the "child . . . within himself," a child whose knowledge of language and literature in his early teens would be the envy of many adults. A careful reading of the Narnia stories will send most children, or their parents, to a good desk dictionary—sometimes even to the unabridged *Oxford English Dictionary.* The following pages offer definitions of unusual terms, possible literary allusions, and other textual notes that are not mentioned in the main text.

The Magician's Nephew

Sherlock Holmes: The fictional detective created by Sir Arthur Conan Doyle (1859–1930).

Bastables: Fictional family created by Edith Nesbit (1828–1924).

Mad wife shut up in attic: Charlotte Brontë, *Jane Eyre* (1847).

Coiner: British slang for a counterfeiter.

Pirate hiding from shipmates: Robert Louis Stevenson, *Treasure Island* (1883).

Cistern: Water storage tank.

Mrs. Lefay: The kindly godmother of the Lefay fragment is replaced here by a sinister godmother. Both call to mind Morgan le Fay, the fairy sister of King Arthur.

Bunk (verb): Slang for run away.

Adept (noun): An expert in occult sciences.

Show the white feather: Give up out of cowardice.

St. Paul's: Cathedral in London.

Minion: Contemptuous term for a servile follower.

The "Mark" of wicked Magicians: Possible allusion to the Mark of Cain (Genesis 4:15) or the Mark of the Antichrist (Revelation 16:2).

Call it Pax: Call a truce, make peace (Latin *pax*).

Hansom: A two-wheeled covered carriage drawn by one horse, named after its inventor.

Sal volatile: Smelling salts.

Land of Youth: Allusion to Irish Tirnanog, "land of the young ones," which Lewis's childhood nurse used to tell him about.

"Colney 'Atch": Cockney for Colney Hatch, an insane asylum in London.

Aslan singing his new song: Psalm 33:3.

Yeomanry: Cavalry unit attached to the British Territorial Army.

Animals from lumps of earth: John Milton's *Paradise Lost,* Book 7, offers a similar creation scene with animals bursting forth from the earth.

Faun: Mythological creature with the body of a man and the horns, pointed ears, tail, and hind legs of a goat.

Satyr: A kind of faun usually associated with riotous merriment.

Naiad: A water nymph.

"My Little Man": Robert Capron, the harsh schoolmaster, referred to the young Lewis as the "little man" in a letter to Lewis's father; thus, this wording underscores Lewis's association of Uncle Andrew with Capron.

"My son, my son": Possible echo of David's lament over Absalom (2 Samuel 18:33).

Curvet: A horse's leap in which the hind legs are raised just before the forelegs touch the ground.

"Is it good?": Possible echo of the phrase "it was good" that is repeated throughout Genesis 1.

Jadis climbing the wall: Echo of John 10:1, in which Jesus says that a shepherd enters a sheepfold by the gate, while a thief climbs the wall. In *Paradise Lost* (Book 4), John Milton pictures Eden as a walled garden, with Satan leaping over its wall.

Multicolored bird in the apple tree: A phoenix, the mythical bird that is consumed by fire every five hundred years and then emerges anew from the ashes. The phoenix is a traditional symbol of immortality.

Aslan's "Well done": Matthew 25:21, 23.

The Lion, the Witch and the Wardrobe

Lamp-post in Lantern Waste: M. A. Manzalaoui, who studied under Lewis, speculates that the image of an isolated lamppost in the middle of woods may have come from a Victorian gas lamppost near Newnham, Cambridge. The lamppost was installed by local officials in the nineteenth century to illuminate a natural skating rink that formed in winters when the River Cam overran its banks. No longer in use, the lamppost now stands by itself in a clearing surrounded by woods, seemingly in the middle of nowhere. Manzalaoui offers no evidence that Lewis knew of this lamppost (Lindskoog, *Journey,* 211–212).

Spare Oom, War Drobe: Lewis is joking about a common mistake called *misdivision* by linguists. He was probably influenced here, perhaps unconsciously, by a scene in Edith Nesbit's "The Aunt and Amabel," in which a little girl discovers a train station to the world of enchantment inside a place called *Bigwardrobeinspareroom.*

Dryads: Tree nymphs.

Silenus: Leader of the satyrs, usually portrayed as a fat, drunken, jolly old man.

Bacchus: Roman god of wine and revelry.

Turkish Delight: British candy, a jellied confection with powdered sugar (not nearly tasty enough to betray one's siblings for). Kathryn Lindskoog (*Journey,* 107) says that some university students in England used to lace their Turkish Delight with hashish. She offers no evidence that Lewis was aware of this practice.

Chatelaine: Mistress of a castle.

"I hear and obey":   The wolf's response on receiving orders is the same as that used by slaves in *The Thousand and One Nights.*

Cair Paravel: In *Collected Letters,* vol. 1, 468, Lewis notes that the word *kaer* is Celtic for "city." It is usually translated "castle."

Stratagem: Clever battle plan.

World Ash Tree: In Norse mythology, the tree representing all creation.

Skirling: A shrill, piercing sound, such as that made by bagpipes.

Mice nibbling Aslan's cords: An allusion to one of Aesop's fables.

The White Stag: Lewis borrows from Celtic lore about the white stag who grants one wish to those who catch him. In the most famous version of the legend, a poor cottager, Sean Kiley, caught the white stag, who gave him one day to decide on his wish. Sean's barren wife wanted to become pregnant; his blind mother wanted her eyesight restored; his impoverished father wanted some financial security. So the young son and husband went to the stag the next day and made one wish: that Sean's mother could gaze upon his newborn son rocking in a cradle of gold.

The Horse and His Boy

Creek: In British usage, a narrow inlet or bay.

Scimitar: Sword with a crescent-shaped blade.

Loquacity: Talkativeness.

Grand Vizier: Chief adviser to a monarch.

Apothegms: Proverbs, practical sayings.

Hastilude: Spear play, games of combat.

Weathercocks: Weather vanes.

Prognostics: Forewarnings.

Scullion: A kitchen helper.

Hermit's view of Luck: Compare to Lewis, *The Four Loves:* "For a Christian, there are, strictly speaking, no chances. A secret Master of Ceremonies has been at work" (126).

Portcullis: Iron grate that slides down in front of a castle door.

Funk: To fail through cowardice.

Pajock: A strutting peacock. The word appeared originally in an early folio of Shakespeare's *Hamlet,* a misprint for *pacock,* a variant of peacock. Hamlet is on the verge of calling someone a "very, very Ass," but instead calls him a "very, very pajock." Early readers did not recognize *pajock* as a misprint, so they thought it was a term of abuse similar to *Ass*. Lewis inserts a literary joke here, as Rabadash will literally become a "very, very Ass."

Estres: Chambers, apartments.

Prince Caspian

Knights Errant: Knights on a quest or in pursuit of adventure.

Dais: Raised platform for seats of honor.

Pomona: Roman goddess of fruits and fruit trees.

Torch: British term for flashlight.

Wars of the Roses: English civil wars between the houses of York and Lancaster (1455–1485).

Theorbo: A lute with two necks.

Aslan's How: A how is an ancient burial mound, hollowed out inside.

Seneschal: Head servant in the household of a nobleman.

Jinn: A shape-shifting spirit in Islamic mythology. (This word was altered in English to *genie*.)

Hauberk: Medieval coat of armor, usually of chain mail.

Lucy called by Aslan in the night: Allusion to the call of Samuel by God (1 Samuel 3:1–20).

Bromios, Bassareus, the Ram: Names for the Greek god Dionysus (Roman Bacchus).

Euan euan eu-oi-oi-oi: A traditional cry at feasts of Bacchus. *Euan* is another name for the god of celebration and *euoi* is a shout of merriment (Ford, 71).

Cantrips: Magic spells.

Tussock: A tuft of grass or ground cover.

Litter: A stretcher for carrying the wounded.

Maenads: Frenzied female attendants of Bacchus.

Bridge of Beruna: This scene is very similar to the destruction of a ship in Ovid's *Metamorphosis,* Book 3 (Ford, 48).

The Voyage of the "Dawn Treader"

Cog: Medieval ship with rounded prow and stern.

Dromond: Large, swift medieval ship.

Carrack: Galleon used as a merchant vessel.

Galleon: Large, two-masted ship originating in Spain.

Queen Mary: British luxury liner.

Republican: As Eustace uses the term, it means "egalitarian."

Trice: "In a trice" means "in an instant."

Jetty: A landing pier.

Postern: Smaller door within a castle's main gate.

Androcles and the lion: Allusion to the story of Androcles, a Roman slave, who removed a thorn from the paw of a lion. Later, when Androcles was thrown into the arena, the lion refused to harm him and both were set free.

Quoits: A game like horseshoes in which rings are thrown at a hanging peg.

Poor Bottom: Bottom was a comic character in Shakespeare's *Midsummer Night's Dream.*

Astrolabe: Early navigational instrument.

Orrery: Device for illustrating the relative position of the planets.

Chronoscope: Precise timepiece.

Theodolind: Lewis may have had in mind a *theodolite,* a portable surveying instrument.

Choriambuses, poisemeters: Whimsical names for fictitious instruments. A *choriambus* is a type of Greek poetic meter; a *poisemeter* would be a device for measuring poetic rhythms.

Poltroonery: Cowardice.

Berries like live coals in the mouth: Allusion to Isaiah 6:6–7.

Kraken: Sea monster from Greek mythology.

Keel-hauled: Dragged under the ship's keel as punishment.

Ulysses and the Sirens: In the *Odyssey,* Odysseus (Ulysses) wants to hear the song of the sirens, beautiful maids whose song lures sailors to their death. He has his crew bind him to the mast and fill their own ears with wax as they sail by the sirens.

Lamb serving a fish breakfast: Echo of Jesus' appearance to his disciples in John, chap. 21.

Bridge Builder: Translation of Pontifex Maximus, an important Roman official in charge of roads, bridges, and aqueducts. Early Christians called Christ "the Pontifex" because he built a bridge between humans and God, between mortal life and immortal.

The Silver Chair

Lions in Trafalgar Square: Stone lions in a famous memorial plaza in London.

Turreted: With towers.

Quay: A dock (pronounced "key").

Forecastle and poop: Raised decks fore and aft in a ship.

Bulwarks: The thick sides of a ship above the upper deck.

Physic: Archaic term for the profession of medicine (hence our term *physician*).

Marches (noun): Border country.

"Vengeance on a witless brute": Echo of Starbuck's advice to Ahab in *Moby-Dick* not to seek "vengeance on a dumb brute" (chap. 36).

Belfry: Bell tower.

Bobaunce: Lewis found this word for boasting in Chaucer (*Collected Letters,* vol. 2, 568).

Cock-shies: Game of throwing stones at a target.

Bivouac: A temporary encampment.

Minotaurs: Mythical creatures with the head of a bull and the body of a man.

Puttees: Coverings for the lower legs.

Possets and comfits: Spiced drinks and candies.

Scullery: Area in a castle where servants prepare food and wash dishes.

Strait: Tight, confined.

Ark: Box to hold precious objects.

Salamanders in fire: Lewis mentions medieval texts referring to gnomes living in the earth and salamanders in fire in *The Discarded Image,* 135.

Leech: An archaic word for a doctor, from their use of leeches to draw blood.

Nine names of Aslan: Echo of the seven names of God recognized by the ancient Hebrews, called The Seven in medieval times.

I will not always be scolding: Psalm 103:9.

Pillar box: A pillar-shaped mailbox.

Aslan weeping over Caspian: An echo of Jesus weeping before the tomb of Lazarus (John, chap. 11).

"They shall see only my back": Allusion to Exodus 33:22–23, in which God will not show Moses his face.

The Last Battle

Panniers: Saddle packs or baskets.

Fell (adjective): Cruel or deadly (as in the phrase *one fell swoop*).

Rive (verb): Archaic word for split (related to *rift*).

Malapert: Impudently bold; saucy.

Miscreant: Evildoer (literally "disbeliever").

Churl: Ill-mannered peasant.

Rilian the Disenchanted: Rilian is disenchanted in the sense that he is freed from the spell of an enchantress.

Tirian and Jewel's rage: An echo of Moses striking down an Egyptian slavemaster (Exodus 2:11–12).

When Narnians spoke to Aslan face to face: Exodus 33:11 mentions God and Moses speaking face to face.

The rock with refreshing waters: See Exodus 20:7–11; 1 Corinthians 10:4.

Susan no longer a friend of Narnia: Lewis explained in a letter that Susan's estrangement from Narnia need not be permanent. She may merely be in a phase of false sophistication in the same way that he was in his own teen years (*Letters to Children*, 67).

They were beginning Chapter One: Lewis admired a remark by Thomas Traherne that all of life was merely the "frontispiece of Eternity" (*Collected Letters*, vol. 1, 914).

NOTES

Page numbers for quotations from the Narnia books are given in *italics* for the HarperCollins paperback editions, published in the United States since 1994. Page numbers for the earlier Collier paperback editions are given in roman type. Biblical quotations are from the King James Version, unless otherwise noted.

Introduction: The Child as Father of the Man

p. xiii   "An almost uniquely persisting": *Collected Letters,* vol. 2, 882.

p. xiv   Most recognized voice: Como, *Reminiscences,* xxi.

"The most sustained achievement": H. Carpenter and M. Prichard, *The Oxford Companion to Children's Literature* (Oxford, U.K.: Oxford University Press, 1984), 370.

"Humanity does not pass": *The Allegory of Love,* 1.

p. xv   Uncomfortable around children: *Abolition of Man,* 29.

"The child who was within himself": Wilson, 221.

"I don't think age matters": *Letters to Children,* 34.

"Youth and age only touch": *That Hideous Strength,* 21.

p. xvi   "Boyish greatness": Schofield, 87.

"When I became a man": "On Three Ways of Writing for Children," *Of Other Worlds,* 25.

Chapter One: The Life of C. S. Lewis

p. 2   "Baby doesn't see": *Letters to Children*, 10.

                   "He is Jacksie": *Letters to Children*, 10.

p. 3   Albert's and Flora's writing: Bresland, 19.

                   "Almost a major character": *Surprised by Joy*, 10.

                   Warren recalls tunnel-like attics: *Letters to Children*, 12.

p. 4   Claire (Lewis) Clapperton's memories: *Letters to Children*, 12–13.

                   "Knights-in-armor" and "dressed animals," imaginary worlds of "India" and "Animal-Land": *Surprised by Joy*, 3.

                   Stories of chivalrous mice: *Surprised by Joy*, 13.

                   "Astonishingly prosaic": *Surprised by Joy*, 15.

p. 5   Lizzie's Irish folktales: Green and Hooper, 21.

                   "Even the exacting memory": *Surprised by Joy*, 5.

                   "Unless we return": "The Poison of Subjectivism," *Christian Reflections*, 81.

p. 6   "The person he loved best": *Prince Caspian, 41*, 37.

                   Memories of Dunluce Castle: *Collected Letters*, vol. 1, 143, 188.

                   "Nearer by twenty centuries": *English Literature*, 26–27.

                   "The learned and the adult": *The Problem of Pain*, 67.

p. 7   "Enormous bliss" of Eden: *Surprised by Joy*, 16.

                   "Unsatisfied desire": *Surprised by Joy*, 17–18.

pp. 7–8   *Northernness* as "cold, spacious": *Surprised by Joy*, 17.

p. 8   Gazing from Little Lea to the hills: *Surprised by Joy*, 7.

"Bad temper": *Lewis Papers,* vol. 3, 89.

p. 10   "As a buffoon than an ogre": *Surprised by Joy,* 31.

p. 11   "We all loved her": *Surprised by Joy,* 59.

"Two frightened urchins": *Surprised by Joy,* 19.

p. 12   "Nearly all that I loved": *Surprised by Joy,* 170.

"Great literary experience": *Collected Letters,* vol. 1, 169.

"Spiritual healing": *Collected Letters,* vol. 1, 936.

p. 13   "Capacity for simple happiness": G. MacDonald, *Phantastes and Lilith* (Grand Rapids, Mich.: Eerdmans, 1964), 43.

"A power of calm endurance": MacDonald, *Phantastes and Lilith,* 180.

MacDonald serves as devotional reading: *All My Road,* 177.

"The quality which enchanted me": *George MacDonald: An Anthology,* 26–27.

p. 15   "Satan Speaks": *Spirits in Bondage,* 3.

p. 17   "The beaten track": *Surprised by Joy,* 203.

p. 18   "Terrible things are happening": *Collected Letters,* vol. 1, 882–883.

p. 19   "The organ of meaning": "Bluspels and Flalansferes," *Selected Literary Essays,* 265.

p. 20   "Intellectual stagnation": *Collected Letters,* vol. 1, 342.

p. 21   Standing room—only lectures: Hart, 3.

"By far the most impressive": Gardner, 424.

"Almost impossible to exaggerate": Keefe, 105.

Chapter Two: The Genesis of Narnia

p. 27   "I feel my zeal": *Collected Letters,* vol. 2, 905–906. Lewis was writing in Latin to an Italian correspondent, Don Giovanni Calabria. The words quoted are an English translation.

p. 28   Most Lewis scholars agree: See Schakel, *"Imagination,"* 40–53, for the most compelling argument for reading the books in the order that they were originally published. See also Adey, 177; Ford, xix–xx; Gibson, 194–195; Hannay, 23–71; Manlove, *Chronicles,* 30–31.

     Lewis agrees to Narnian chronological order: *Letters to Children,* 68.

     Lewis to Hooper on correct order: Hooper, *Dragons,* 32.

p. 29   "The *Lion* all began": *Of Other Worlds,* 42.

     "Delightful" evacuees: *Collected Letters,* vol. 2, 451.

     "This book is about four children": Green and Hooper, 238.

p. 30   "In the tradition of E. Nesbit": Green and Hooper, 238.

     Lewis losing a debate: Wilson, 210–214; see also Carpenter, 216–222.

     Purtill's rebuttal: See Walker and Patrick, 45–53.

p. 31   "The Wood That Time Forgot": Green and Hooper, 239–240.

p. 32   Tolkien had not heard of the atomic bomb: "On Criticism," *Of Other Worlds,* 49.

p. 33   "'Creation' as applied": *Collected Letters,* vol. 2, 555.

     "Everything began with images": "Sometimes Fairy Stories May Say Best What's to Be Said," *Of Other Worlds,* 36.

Lewis's letter on his choice of a lion: Hooper, *Companion*, 426.

"Always winter": *The Lion, the Witch and the Wardrobe, 20, 16*.

pp. 33–34   White Witch as the daughter of Lilith: *The Lion, the Witch and the Wardrobe, 88,* 77. Lewis also referred to the temptress Ayesha in Rider Haggard's *She* (1887) as a "white witch" (*Letters to Children,* 29).

p. 34   White Witch as Circe; "The same Archetype": Unpublished letter, quoted in Schakel, *Reading,* 9.

"Fairy tale liberates Archetypes": "On Three Ways of Writing for Children," *Of Other Worlds,* 27.

"No merely physical strangeness": "On Stories," *Of Other Worlds,* 12.

p. 35   Maud Barfield's concern: *Collected Letters,* vol. 2, 942.

Boy who chopped wardrobe: Hooper, "Preface," in Lindskoog, *Lion,* 14.

p. 36   The Lefay fragment is printed in full in Hooper, *Dragons,* 48–65.

p. 38   Mrs. Lefay as burlesque: Hooper, *Dragons,* 66.

p. 39   Mrs. Lefay in *The Magician's Nephew: 18–22,* 16–19.

"Aslan pulled": Hooper, *Companion,* 404.

p. 40   Alternate titles for *Prince Caspian:* Green and Hooper, 243.

p. 41   "Parachronic state": *That Hideous Strength,* 226.

"Other Natures": *Miracles,* 14–15.

p. 42   Literary and spiritual implications: See Gibson, 157–159, for a fuller discussion of parallel time streams.

Lewis's time line of Narnian history: Hooper, *Dragons,* 41–44.

"Time is a defect of reality": *Collected Letters,* vol. 2, 915.

"With the Lord one day": 2 Peter 3:8 (RSV). Lewis's letter offered a paraphrase.

p. 43   Lewis's notes for *The Voyage of the "Dawn Treader"*: Hooper, *Companion,* 403.

p. 46   "Dim, purple kind of smell": *The Voyage of the "Dawn Treader,"* 206, 164.

"Otherworld Quests": G. Ashe, *Land to the West: St. Brendan's Voyage to America* (New York: Viking, 1962), 61.

p. 47   "The spiritual life": Hooper, *Companion,* 426.

"Anyone in our world": *Letters to Children,* 45.

"Where sky and water meet": *The Voyage of the "Dawn Treader,"* 22, 16.

p. 48   Reepicheep is the Dawn Treader: Gibson, 172.

pp. 49-50   Source of the name Aslan: *Letters to Children,* 29.

p. 50   Calormen influenced by *The Thousand and One Nights*: Unpublished letter, April 13, 1953.

Lewis didn't like *The Thousand and One Nights*: "On Juvenile Tastes," *Of Other Worlds,* 39.

p. 51   Middle Eastern customs on hair coloring: E. W. Lane (trans.), *The Arabian Nights' Entertainments, or The Thousand and One Nights.* New York: Pickwick, 1927. See notes on pp. 934, 1099, 1259.

p. 52   "Captivity captive": Ephesians 4:9–10.

Christ preaching to the spirits in prison: 1 Peter 3:19.

p. 53   "Same crew": *The Silver Chair,* 61, 52.

"Those Northern Witches": *The Silver Chair, 240,* 201.

Puddleglum drawn from Paxford: Hooper, *Dragons,* 81.

p. 55 Shift the Ape as a Narnian Antichrist: *Letters to Children,* 93.

p. 57 Greeves borrowed Sherlock Holmes books: *Collected Letters,* vol. 2, 34.

Lewis more partial to Edith Nesbit: *Surprised by Joy,* 14.

"Throttled by a stiff Eton collar": *Surprised by Joy,* 22.

Not as an ogre: *Surprised by Joy,* 31.

Capron would make a memorable villain: *Collected Letters,* vol. 1, 208.

p. 58 Comparisons of appearances of Robert Capron and Andrew Ketterley: *Lewis Papers,* vol. 3, 36, 41; *The Magician's Nephew, 5, 13–14, 26–27, 40, 132;* 4, 11–12, 23–24, 36, 112.

Comparison of origins and speech of Robert Capron and Andrew Ketterley: *Lewis Papers,* vol. 3, 36, 92; *The Magician's Nephew, 78, 83, 90, 93, 95, 111, 114, 221;* 67, 71, 77, 79, 81, 94, 97, 186.

p. 59 Scene Lewis admired in *King Solomon's Mines:* "De Audiendis Poetis," in *Studies in Medieval and Renaissance Literature,* 12.

Lewis called Jadis a white witch: *Letters to Children,* 41.

pp. 59–60 Lewis's favorable comments on Blackwood's books: *Collected Letters,* vol. 1, 192, 224–225, 312.

p. 60 "Good romancer into a bad mystic": *Collected Letters,* vol. 1, 375.

"Oh, I have never read": *Collected Letters,* vol. 1, 162.

"He realized vividly": A. Blackwood, *The Education of Uncle Paul* (London: Macmillan, 1931), 170–171.

p. 61   "'Between Yesterday and Tomorrow'": Blackwood, *Education*, 201.

"Wanderlust of the spirit": Blackwood, *Education*, 201–202.

"Fine woman": Blackwood, *Education*, 302.

p. 62   "It's not the sort of place": *The Magician's Nephew*, *33*, 30.

Chapter Three: The Spiritual Vision of the Narnia Chronicles

p. 63   "Extraordinarily kind": *The Pilgrim's Regress*, 22.

"Grandfather in heaven": *The Problem of Pain*, 28.

p. 64   "Pure moonshine": "Sometimes Fairy Stories May Say Best What's to Be Said," *Of Other Worlds*, 36.

"An imaginary world": "Sometimes Fairy Stories," *Of Other Worlds*, 37.

"You are mistaken": *Letters to Children*, 44–45.

p. 65   "That which is supreme": R. Otto, *The Idea of the Holy* (J. W. Harvey, trans.; London: Oxford University Press, 1923), 10. For a fuller discussion of Lewis's interest in mysticism, see Downing, *Region*.

p. 66   Examples of the numinous: *The Problem of Pain*, 6.

p. 67   "Who said anything": *The Lion, the Witch and the Wardrobe*, *86*, 75–76.

"People who have not been in Narnia": *The Lion, the Witch and the Wardrobe*, *140*, 123.

"The numinous is luminous": E. Bevan, *Symbolism and Belief* (London: Allen & Unwin, 1938), 130.

"Pretty elderly lion": *Prince Caspian*, *132*, 122.

"The same yesterday, today, and forever": Hebrews 13:8.

p. 68   "Fiery brightness": *The Horse and His Boy, 178,* 160.

Aslan's appearance to Emeth: *The Last Battle, 204,* 164.

Life Force a "Tame God": *Mere Christianity,* 34, 172.

p. 69   "It is as if the sun": *The Last Battle, 32, 25.*

"Aslan is not a tame lion": *The Lion, the Witch and the Wardrobe, 200,* 180

"Calling God good": Quoted in D. Baumgardt, *The Great Western Mystics: Their Lasting Significance* (New York: Columbia University Press, 1961), 44.

"The Divine 'goodness' differs from ours": *The Problem of Pain,* 27.

"Mere power": *Miracles,* 94.

p. 70   Aslan's answer suggests the Trinity: *Letters of C. S. Lewis,* 486; *The Horse and His Boy, 176,* 159.

Milton's mistake in portraying God the Father: *A Preface to Paradise Lost,* 130–131.

p. 71   "Do not dare not to dare": *The Horse and His Boy, 215,* 193.

Christ's words to doubting Thomas: John 20:26–28.

Hooper on *spirit: Companion,* 440.

Aslan's breath brings statues to life: *The Lion, the Witch and the Wardrobe, 183–185,* 164–166.

Sculptor's studio: *Mere Christianity,* 139–140.

p. 72   Faith of the Hebrews: Bevan, *Symbolism and Belief,* 20.

"Great and beautiful": *The Last Battle, 228,* 183.

p. 73   Creation of Narnia: *The Magician's Nephew, 116–119,* 99–101.

Creation of Talking Beasts: *The Magician's Nephew,* *136–139,* 115–117.

"The old definition": *Perelandra,* 207.

p. 74   "An anguish, an alienation": *Letters to Malcolm,* 44.

God as Tragic Creator: *Letters to Malcolm,* 91.

p. 75   "My son, my son": *The Magician's Nephew, 168,* 142.

p. 76   "Come in by the gold gates": *The Magician's Nephew,* *187,* 157.

Principle of Vicariousness: *Miracles,* 122–123.

pp. 76–77   "It [is] the rule": *Collected Letters,* vol. 2,, 953, italics in original.

p. 77   "He saved others, himself he cannot save": Matthew 27:42.

"Evil will come": *The Magician's Nephew, 161,* 136.

Law engraved on the Stone Table: Lewis confirmed in a letter that this was intended to remind readers of Moses' table (as the KJV refers to the tablets).

p. 78   Pauline Baynes didn't think of Christ: Hooper, *Companion,* 625.

Theological questions about atonement: Taliaferro, 78–79.

"You must not confuse": *Collected Letters,* vol. 2, 914.

pp. 78–79   "Real help": *Collected Letters,* vol. 2, 479.

p. 79   "To act the part of a kinsman": Sister Penelope, *Windows on Jerusalem: A Study in the Mystery of Redemption* (London: Pax House, 1941), 52.

"Really splendid account": *Collected Letters,* vol. 2, 479.

"Completely repudiated": Sister Penelope, *Windows,* 56.

"The whole flood"; "Before the Cross": Sister Penelope, *Windows,* 56.

"Can anything be done": *The Lion, the Witch and the Wardrobe, 141,* 124.

p. 80   "'It isn't Narnia, you know'": *The Voyage of the "Dawn Treader," 269,* 215.

"This was the very reason": *The Voyage of the "Dawn Treader," 270,* 216.

"Has there ever been anyone": *Letters to Children,* 32.

p. 81   "Courage, dear heart": *The Voyage of the "Dawn Treader," 201,* 160.

"A dream (if it was a dream)": *The Last Battle, 53,* 42.

pp. 81–82   "I don't think that matters": *Letters of C. S. Lewis,* 432.

p. 82   Aslan more a witness than a judge: Ford, 171.

p. 83   Wave/particle conundrum: *Letters,* 433.

Saved by grace through faith: Ephesians 2:8, 9.

p. 84   "To be the one kind of creature": *Mere Christianity,* 86.

"There are only two kinds of people": *The Great Divorce,* 72.

"Surpassed in beauty": *The Last Battle, 204,* 164.

p. 85   Lewis's letters about Christ's portrayal of judgment: See, for example, *Letters* (1988), 418.

Christ's portrayal of judgment: Matthew 25:31–46.

"We do know that no man": *Mere Christianity,* 65.

"I think every prayer": *Collected Letters,* vol. 2, 135, n. 9.

"All find what they truly seek": *The Last Battle, 206,* 165.

pp. 85–86   Lewis's letter to Laurence's mother: *Letters to Children,* 52–53.

p. 86   "The Narnia stories reveal": Sayer, 319.

"The figure of Aslan": Quoted in Sayer, 319.

p. 87   "I am sure Aslan knows best": *Letters to Children*, 69; see also 75, 76.

Chapter Four: Moral Psychology

p. 89   "Still—a robin you know": *The Lion, the Witch and the Wardrobe*, 67, 59.

pp. 89–90   "When Adam's flesh": *The Lion, the Witch and the Wardrobe*, 87, 76.

p. 90   "Fairy tales"; "nonsense": *Prince Caspian*, 43, 39.

Children's stories less escapist: *Surprised by Joy*, 35.

"Doctrine of objective value": *The Abolition of Man*, 29.

p. 91   "It is the Way": *The Abolition of Man*, 28.

"Resounding lie": "The Poison of Subjectivism," *Christian Reflections*, 77.

p. 92   "Old sinner": *The Magician's Nephew*, 202, 171.

"Horrid school": *The Lion, the Witch and the Wardrobe*, 197, 177.

"In which everything": *Surprised by Joy*, 71.

"Very horrid": *Letters to Children*, 102.

p. 93   Edmund's bad traits: *The Lion, the Witch and the Wardrobe*, 2, 4, 28; 2, 4, 23.

"Rebellion of the will": *Collected Letters*, vol. 2, 929.

pp. 93–94   Peter apologizes: *The Lion, the Witch and the Wardrobe*, 60, 51.

p. 94   "Self-satisfied prigs": *The Lion, the Witch and the Wardrobe*, 62, 53.

Responses to the name Aslan: *The Lion, the Witch and the Wardrobe*, 74–75, 64–65.

pp. 94–95   Responses of Digory and Frank: *The Magician's Nephew, 116–117,* 99–100.

p. 95   "The complete anti-God state of mind": *Mere Christianity,* 109.

Bree's and Hwin's different responses: *The Horse and His Boy, 215,* 193.

p. 96   "Deep down inside him": *The Lion, the Witch and the Wardrobe, 97,* 86.

pp. 96–97   Aslan questioning Jill: *The Silver Chair, 22–23,* 18–19.

p. 97   Aslan questioning Digory: *The Magician's Nephew, 161,* 136.

pp. 97–98   Edmund's fantasies: *The Lion, the Witch and the Wardrobe, 98,* 87.

p. 98   "Annihilates space": *Surprised by Joy,* 157.

"Wars and industrialisms": *Out of the Silent Planet,* 70.

"The commercial possibilities": *The Magician's Nephew, 131,* 111.

p. 99   "A country worth living in": *The Last Battle, 38,* 30.

"Terrible and sad and noble": *The Lion, the Witch and the Wardrobe, 104,* 91.

p. 100   "For the first time": *The Lion, the Witch and the Wardrobe, 128,* 113. As Paul F. Ford notes, this phrase in the chronicles often signals a moment of spiritual transformation (*Companion,* 192–193).

Festivity turned to statuary: *Letters to Children,* 53.

"Ruthless, sleepless": *The Screwtape Letters,* ix.

p. 101   Contrasts of selfishness and caring: *The Magician's Nephew, 23–24, 71;* 21, 61; *The Horse and His Boy, 71,* 40; *The Silver Chair, 165,* 138.

"A great leap": *The Lion, the Witch and the Wardrobe, 129,* 114.

p. 102   "It was a conversation": *The Lion, the Witch and the Wardrobe, 152,* 135.

Aslan's replies: *The Voyage of the "Dawn Treader," 270,* 216; *The Horse and His Boy, 216,* 194.

p. 103   "What is that to thee?": John 21:22.

Lewis quoted this verse: *Mere Christianity,* 7.

"Peter did not feel very brave": *The Lion, the Witch and the Wardrobe, 144,* 127.

"Courage is not simply": *The Screwtape Letters,* Letter 29.

p. 104   "Well done": *Prince Caspian, 162,* 148.

p. 105   Edmund's reassurance of Eustace: *The Voyage of the "Dawn Treader," 117,* 91–92.

pp. 105–106   Lewis's letter about stories with a point: *Letters to Children,* 35.

Chapter Five: Classical and Medieval Elements

p. 107   Titles of Renaissance lectures: *Collected Letters,* vol. 2, 246.

"An imaginary entity": *Collected Letters,* vol. 2, 475.

p. 108   "Great Divide": *"De Descriptione Temporum," Selected Literary Essays,* 3–10.

pp. 108–109   Continuity between pagan and Christian: *The Discarded Image,* 46–47.

p. 109   "The childhood of religion": *Surprised by Joy,* 235.

"I think the thrill": *Collected Letters,* vol. 2, 12–13.

pp. 109–110   "A real though unfocused gleam": *Miracles,* 139.

p. 110   Mixing of Christian and classical: "Hero and Leander," *Selected Literary Essays,* 65.

"A thousand years of theology": *English Literature,* 20.

He avoided the term *Renaissance: English Literature,* 55.

"The barrier between those two ages": "*De Descriptione Temporum,*" *Selected Literary Essays,* 2.

p. 111 Sphericity and Smallness of Earth: *The Problem of Pain,* 3; *Miracles,* 50; *The Discarded Image,* 97; "Imagination and Thought in the Middle Ages," *Studies in Medieval and Renaissance Literature,* 46–47.

"I think we have had enough": *The Voyage of the "Dawn Treader,"* 62, 48.

pp. 111–112 Lewis on democracy: "A Reply to Professor Haldane," *Of Other Worlds,* 81.

p. 112 "Govertisement": "*De Descriptione Temporum,*" *Selected Literary Essays,* 8.

Distortions of the natural order: *A Preface to Paradise Lost,* 76.

p. 113 "Rough magic": *The Voyage of the "Dawn Treader,"* 174, 137.

pp. 113–114 "You are the King of Narnia": *The Voyage of the "Dawn Treader,"* 261, 209.

p. 114 Necessity of democracy: "Membership," *The Weight of Glory and Other Addresses,* 37.

"Dressed animals" and "knights in armor": *Surprised by Joy,* 13.

p. 115 "The greatest thing": *Collected Letters,* vol. 1, 104.

Praise for *Sir Gawain: Collected Letters,* vol. 1, 180. Lewis was reading a prose translation by E.J.B. Kirtlan (1912).

"The perfect poem of chivalry": *Collected Letters,* vol. 1, 187.

"The Quest of Bleheris": Manuscript in the Bodleian Library, Oxford (MS. Eng. lett. c. 220/5 fols. 5–43). Copies of the manuscript are housed at the Marion E. Wade Center, Wheaton College, Wheaton, Illinois. For a fuller discussion of this fragment, see Downing, *Reluctant Convert*, chap. 4.

p.117   "Red rampant lion": *The Lion, the Witch and the Wardrobe, 138,* 122.

p. 118   "Ad-hominable": *Prince Caspian, 222,* 173.

"Waters-meet"; "heart's-scald": *The Horse and His Boy, 148, 191;* 134, 171.

Naught; hastilude: *The Horse and His Boy, 62, 68;* 57, 62.

p. 119   "I am confounded": *Prince Caspian, 222,* 202.

"One of the great Christian ideas": *Mere Christianity,* 107.

Aslan's qualities like those of the Grail: Hooper, *Dragons,* 95.

pp. 119–120   "It is interesting to notice": *The Allegory of Love,* 23–24.

p. 120   "You will find people": *The Abolition of Man,* 87.

"Part of the furniture of romance": *English Literature,* 8.

p. 121   Merlin as an injured soul: *That Hideous Strength,* 265.

"Some magic in the house": *The Lion, the Witch and the Wardrobe, 57,* 49.

p. 122   "Strong magic": *Letters to Malcolm,* 103–104.

"A very imperfect magician": *Prince Caspian, 58,* 53.

"Not a proper study for princes": *Prince Caspian, 58,* 53.

"Rough magic": *The Voyage of the "Dawn Treader," 174,* 137.

Prospero's renunciation: *The Tempest*, V, 1, 50–51.

p. 123   "Rather rot": *The Silver Chair*, 7, 6.

"High and lonely destiny": *The Magician's Nephew, 21,* 18.

"There is something": *The Abolition of Man*, 87–88.

p. 124   "Ye shall be as gods": Genesis 3:5.

Magic and astrology were never allied: *English Literature*, 6.

Medieval view of astrology: "Imagination and Thought in the Middle Ages," *Studies in Medieval and Renaissance Literature*, 55–56.

"A prophet and a stargazer": *Prince Caspian, 81,* 73.

p. 125   "The great lords of the upper sky": *Prince Caspian, 50,* 45–46.

Primum mobile pictured as a girl: "Imagination and Thought in the Middle Ages," *Studies in Medieval and Renaissance Literature*, 60.

"Are to be conceived": "Imagination and Thought in the Middle Ages," *Studies in Medieval and Renaissance Literature*, 60.

Stars had life, intelligence: *The Discarded Image*, 93.

pp. 125–126   "Once more tread the great dance"; "Even in your world": *The Voyage of the "Dawn Treader," 226,* 180. See A. E. McGrath, *Christian Theology: An Introduction* (London: Blackwell, 1997), 512–513, for a discussion of substance versus accident.

p. 126   "All the stars were falling": *The Last Battle, 189,* 151.

Discussion of the medieval model of the cosmos: *The Discarded Image*, 216–223.

Chapter Six: What's in a Narnian Name?

p. 129   "His Excellenz": *Collected Letters*, vol. 1, 463.

               "Old Air Balloon": Bresland, 37.

               "Galahad": *Collected Letters*, vol. 1, 115.

               "Suit his character": *Collected Letters*, vol. 1, 240.

p. 130   Maleldil: For a discussion of differing interpretations
               of the name Maleldil, see Downing, *Planets in Peril*, 41.

               Liquidity of the name Maleldil: *Letters of C. S. Lewis*,
               476.

p. 131   Yggdrasil: Not named but called "the World Ash Tree"
               on page 138 of pre-1994 American editions of *The
               Lion, the Witch and the Wardrobe*.

               Narnia in Tacitus and Livy: Tacitus, *Annals* 3:9; Livy,
               History 10:10, 27:9.

pp. 131–132   Frank: *Studies in Words*, 117–124.

p. 132   Emeth: *Reflections on the Psalms*, 60–61.

               "Puddle glum": *English Literature*, 256.

pp. 132–133   John Jewel: *English Literature*, 41, 306–307. In his novel
               That Hideous Strength, Lewis included another character
               named Jewel, a faculty member who ineffectually tries
               to oppose the insidious "Progressive Element" at Brac-
               ton College.

p. 133   Tirian and Jewel's attack: *The Last Battle*, 25, 20.

               "I have come home at last!": *The Last Battle*, 213, 171.

               "I must keep alive": *Mere Christianity*, 120.

               Cornelius Agrippa: *English Literature*, 8–13.

pp. 133–134   "The Lady of the Green Kirtle": *The Silver Chair*, 91,
               76.

p. 134   "Green as poison": *The Silver Chair*, 57, 49.

"Prunes and prisms!": Allusion noted in Ford, 336.

p. 135   "Clear Hyaline": J. Milton, *Paradise Lost,* Book 7, line 619.

"Living pogo-sticks": Gibson, 178.

p. 136   Names of fauns: Ford, 184. Though I'm uncertain about several of Paul F. Ford's derivations of faun's names, I am indebted to his indispensable *Companion to Narnia* for sources noted throughout this chapter.

Meaning of Tash: Sammons, 159; Ford, 407.

p. 137   "I am always playing": *Letters of C. S. Lewis,* 476.

"In love with syllables": *Letters to Children,* 108.

p. 139   Strawberry's name: Ford, 192.

"Great glen or wooded gorge": *Prince Caspian, 81,* 73.

p. 140   Lewis owned a cat named Ginger: *Letters to an American Lady,* 69.

"I'm a beast": *Prince Caspian, 184,* 168.

p. 141   "Cruels and Hags": *The Lion, the Witch and the Wardrobe, 165,* 148.

Lady who turned into a grumble: *The Great Divorce,* 74.

Wooses: Ford, 447.

p. 142   Villain: *Studies in Words,* 117–124.

Original English editions of the Narnia chronicles: The HarperCollins editions published in the United States beginning in 1994 return to the texts of the original English editions.

pp. 142–143 Pevensey as a pen name: *Collected Letters,* vol. 2, 911.

p. 143   Peter and the keys: *The Last Battle, 197,* 157. See Matthew 16:19.

p. 144   Jill Flewett's film role: *Collected Letters,* vol. 2, 1035.

"But who are you?": *The Silver Chair, 37,* 31.

"A fop, a cad, and a snob": *Surprised by Joy,* 68.

"Coarse, brainless English schoolboys": *Collected Letters,* vol. 1, 59.

"A monster cut off": *The Voyage of the "Dawn Treader," 98,* 76.

p. 145   "Eustace's character": *The Voyage of the "Dawn Treader," 107,* 83.

"Began to be a different boy": *The Voyage of the "Dawn Treader," 119,* 93.

"Conceited ass": *Collected Letters,* vol. 1, 878; *The Voyage of the "Dawn Treader," 117,* 91.

p. 146   "There seems to be no end": *Collected Letters,* vol. 1, 878–879.

"Throw yourself down safely": *The Pilgrim's Regress,* 168. See Downing, *Region,* chap. 3, for a fuller discussion of this phrase in Augustine's *Confessions.*

"His name unfortunately": *The Silver Chair, 3,* 3.

Chapter Seven: Lewis's Literary Artistry

p. 148   "Making or Glimpsing": J.R.R. Tolkien, "On Fairy-Stories," *Essays Presented to Charles Williams* (Grand Rapids, Mich.: Eerdmans, 1977), 63.

"A children's book": *The Nation,* Apr. 14, 1956. Quoted in L. Carter, *Tolkien: A Look Behind "The Lord of the Rings"* (New York: Ballantine, 1969), 3.

p. 149   Lewis recommended "On Fairy-Stories": Glover 30, 37.

"Longing for a form": "Sometimes Fairy Stories May Say Best What's to Be Said," *Of Other Worlds,* 35.

"Outside the range": Quoted in H. Carpenter, *Tolkien: A Biography* (New York: Ballantine, 1977), 227.

p. 150   "I am almost inclined": "On Three Ways of Writing for Children," *Of Other Worlds,* 24.

p. 151   "My secret, imaginative life": *Surprised by Joy,* 78.

"Some people just don't understand": *Letters of C. S. Lewis,* 445.

Narrator as important character: Schakel, "Imagination," 88. Pages 70–88 of this work provide a thorough, careful analysis of Lewis's narrative techniques.

"Giants of any sort": *The Lion, the Witch and the Wardrobe, 187,* 167.

pp. 151–152 Visit the cave from Underland: *The Silver Chair, 257,* 217.

p. 152   Narrator talking to Lucy: *The Voyage of the "Dawn Treader," 265,* 212.

"You need not wonder": *The Magician's Nephew, 98,* 83.

Narrator's interjections: *The Lion, the Witch and the Wardrobe, 12, 82;* 10, 70.

"And, oh, the cry": *The Lion, the Witch and the Wardrobe, 198,* 178.

"I hope you have": *The Horse and His Boy, 185,* 166.

Explaining Jill's vista to the reader: *The Silver Chair, 14–15,* 11–12.

"And for us": *The Last Battle, 228,* 184.

p. 154   "Fairy tales are not responsible": G. K. Chesterton, *Tremendous Trifles* (New York: Dodd, Mead, 1946), 129–130.

"Death, violence, wounds": "On Three Ways of Writing for Children," *Of Other Worlds,* 31.

pp. 154–155   Lewis's concern about "The Dark Island": *Letters to Children*, 33–34.

p. 155   Lewis's revisions of "The Dark Island": See Ford, 125, 457.

"Tear for tear": *The Horse and His Boy, 216*, 194.

p. 156   "A repressed fund of indignation": *Collected Letters*, vol. 1, 950.

pp. 156–157   Filmer on Lucy and Mrs. Beaver: Filmer, *Fiction*, 105–107.

p. 157   "As fascinating (and infuriating)": *Surprised by Joy*, 200.

p. 158   Women's memories of Lewis: Schofield, 54–55, 57, 62.

pp. 158–159   Sexist remarks of bad characters: *The Magician's Nephew, 28, 25; The Lion, the Witch and the Wardrobe, 32, 26; Prince Caspian, 196,* 179; *The Horse and His Boy, 125,* 112.

p. 159   "Demonization of Islam": Andrew Blake, quoted in González, 51.

pp. 159–160   "Renegade dwarf"; "creature can't help": *Prince Caspian, 90,* 82.

p. 160   Tashbaan in the New Narnia: *The Last Battle, 225,* 181.

pp. 160–161   Reviewers' comments: Hooper, *Companion*, 449–451.

p. 161   "Undeceptions": *Selected Literary Essays*, 177.

pp. 161-162   "Desire for our own far-off country"; "Do you think I am trying to weave a spell?": *The Weight of Glory and Other Addresses*, 4–5.

p. 162   "A longing": "On Three Ways of Writing for Children," *Of Other Worlds*, 29–30.

BIBLIOGRAPHY

Books by C. S. Lewis

The Abolition of Man. New York: Macmillan, 1973. (Originally published 1943.)

All My Road Before Me: The Diary of C. S. Lewis, 1922–1927. (Walter Hooper, ed.). San Diego, Calif.: Harcourt Brace Jovanovich, 1991.

The Allegory of Love. London: Oxford University Press, 1973. (Originally published 1936.)

Christian Reflections. (Walter Hooper, ed.). Grand Rapids, Mich.: Eerdmans, 1973.

The Collected Letters of C. S. Lewis. Vol. 1: *Family Letters 1905–1931.* (Walter Hooper, ed.). London: HarperCollins, 2000.

The Collected Letters of C. S. Lewis. Vol. 2: *Books, Broadcasts, and the War, 1931–1949.* (Walter Hooper, ed.). London: HarperCollins, 2004.

The Discarded Image. Cambridge, U.K.: Cambridge University Press, 1971. (Originally published 1964.)

Dymer. London: J. M. Dent, 1926. Reprinted New York: Macmillan, 1950.

English Literature in the Sixteenth Century, Excluding Drama. Vol. 3 of *Oxford History of English Literature.* Oxford, U.K.: Clarendon Press, 1954.

An Experiment in Criticism. Cambridge, U.K.: Cambridge University Press, 1961.

Fern-Seed and Elephants and Other Essays on Christianity. (Walter Hooper, ed.). New York: Collins/Fountain, 1977.

The Four Loves. New York: Harcourt Brace Jovanovich, 1960.

George MacDonald: An Anthology. (C. S. Lewis, ed.). Garden City, N.Y.: Doubleday, 1962.

God in the Dock: Essays on Theology and Ethics. (Walter Hooper, ed.). Grand Rapids, Mich.: Eerdmans, 1970.

The Great Divorce. New York: Fontana, 1972. (Originally published 1946.)

A Grief Observed. London: Faber and Faber, 1961.

The Horse and His Boy. New York: Collier Books, 1970. (Originally published 1954.)

The Last Battle. New York: Collier Books, 1970. (Originally published 1956.)

Letters: C. S. Lewis/Don Giovanni Calabria. (Martin Moynihan, ed. and trans.). Ann Arbor, Mich.: Servant Books, 1989.

Letters of C. S. Lewis. With a memoir by W. H. Lewis, ed. (Rev. and enlarged ed.; Walter Hooper, ed.). London: HarperCollins, 1988.

Letters to an American Lady. (Clyde S. Kilby, ed.). Grand Rapids, Mich.: Eerdmans, 1967.

Letters to Children. (Lyle W. Dorsett and Marjorie Lamp Mead, eds.). New York: Macmillan, 1985.

Letters to Malcolm: Chiefly on Prayer. New York: Harcourt Brace Jovanovich, 1964.

The Lion, the Witch, and the Wardrobe. New York: Collier Books, 1970. (Originally published 1950.)

The Magician's Nephew. New York: Collier Books, 1970. (Originally published 1955.)

Mere Christianity. New York: Macmillan, 1969. (Originally published 1952.)

Miracles: A Preliminary Study. New York: Macmillan, 1968. (Originally published 1947.)

Narrative Poems. (Walter Hooper, ed.). London: Geoffrey Bles, 1969.

Of Other Worlds: Essays and Stories. (Walter Hooper, ed.). New York: Harcourt Brace Jovanovich, 1975.

On Stories and Other Essays on Literature. New York: Harcourt Brace Jovanovich, 1982.

Out of the Silent Planet. New York: Macmillan, 1968. (Originally published 1938.)

Perelandra. New York: Macmillan, 1968. (Originally published 1943.)

The Personal Heresy: A Controversy. London: Oxford University Press, 1965. (Originally published 1939.)

The Pilgrim's Regress. New York: Harcourt Brace Jovanovich, 1960. (Originally published 1933.)

Poems. (Walter Hooper, ed.). New York: Harcourt Brace Jovanovich, 1964.

A Preface to Paradise Lost. London: Oxford University Press, 1970. (Originally published 1942).

Present Concerns. (Walter Hooper, ed.). San Diego, Calif.: Harcourt Brace Jovanovich, 1987.

Prince Caspian: The Return to Narnia. New York: Collier Books, 1970. (Originally published 1951.)

The Problem of Pain. London: HarperCollins, 1972. (Originally published 1940.)

Reflections on the Psalms. New York: Harcourt Brace Jovanovich, 1982. (Originally published 1958.)

Rehabilitations and Other Essays. London: Oxford University Press, 1939.

The Screwtape Letters. New York: Macmillan, 1960. (Originally published 1942.)

Screwtape Proposes a Toast and Other Pieces. London: HarperCollins, 1970.

Selected Literary Essays. (Walter Hooper, ed.). Cambridge, U.K.: Cambridge University Press, 1966.

The Silver Chair. New York: Collier Books, 1970. (Originally published 1953.)

Spenser's Images of Life. (A. Fowler, ed.). Cambridge, U.K.: Cambridge University Press, 1967.

Spirits in Bondage: A Cycle of Lyrics. New York: Harcourt Brace Jovanovich, 1984. (Originally published 1919.)

Studies in Medieval and Renaissance Literature. (Walter Hooper. ed.). Cambridge, U.K.: Cambridge University Press, 1969.

Studies in Words. Cambridge, U.K.: Cambridge University Press, 1960.

Surprised by Joy: The Shape of My Early Life. New York: Harcourt Brace Jovanovich, 1955.

That Hideous Strength: A Modern Fairy-Tale for Grown-Ups. New York: Macmillan, 1968. (Originally published 1945.)

They Stand Together: The Letters of C. S. Lewis to Arthur Greeves (1914–1963). (Walter Hooper, ed.). New York: Macmillan, 1979.

Till We Have Faces. Grand Rapids, Mich.: Eerdmans, 1966. (Originally published 1956.)

The Voyage of the "Dawn Treader." New York: Collier Books, 1970. (Originally published 1952.)

The Weight of Glory and Other Addresses. Grand Rapids, Mich.: Eerdmans, 1965. (Originally published 1949.)

The World's Last Night and Other Essays. New York: Harcourt Brace Jovanovich, 1960.

Biographies and Biographical Materials

Barfield, Owen. *Owen Barfield on C. S. Lewis.* (G. B. Tennyson, ed.). Middletown, Conn.: Wesleyan University Press, 1989.

Bresland, Ronald W. *The Backward Glance: C. S. Lewis and Ireland.* Belfast, Northern Ireland: The Queen's University of Belfast, 1999.

Carpenter, Humphrey. *The Inklings: C. S. Lewis, J. R. R. Tolkien, Charles Williams, and Their Friends.* Boston: Houghton Mifflin, 1979.

Como, James T. (ed.). *"C. S. Lewis at the Breakfast Table" and other Reminiscences.* New York: Macmillan, 1979.

Dorsett, Lyle W. *And God Came In: The Extraordinary Story of Joy Davidman: Her Life and Marriage to C. S. Lewis.* New York: Macmillan, 1983.

Downing, David C. *The Most Reluctant Convert: C. S. Lewis's Journey to Faith.* Downers Grove, Ill.: InterVarsity Press, 2002.

Gardner, Helen. "Clive Staples Lewis, 1898–1963." *Proceedings of the British Academy,* 1965, *51,* 417–428.

Gibb, Jocelyn (ed.). *Light on C. S. Lewis.* New York: Harcourt, Brace and World, 1965.

Gilbert, Douglas, and Kilby, Clyde S. *C. S. Lewis: Images of His World.* Grand Rapids, Mich.: Eerdmans, 1973.

Graham, David, ed. *We Remember C. S. Lewis: Essays and Memoirs.* Nashville, Tenn.: Broadman & Holman, 2001.

Green, Roger Lancelyn, and Hooper, Walter. *C. S. Lewis: A Biography.* New York: Harcourt Brace Jovanovich, 1974.

Gresham, Douglas. *Lenten Lands.* London: HarperCollins, 1989.

Hooper, Walter. *Through Joy and Beyond: A Pictorial Biography of C. S. Lewis.* New York: Macmillan, 1982.

Keefe, Carolyn (ed.). *C. S. Lewis: Speaker and Teacher.* Grand Rapids, Mich.: Zondervan, 1971.

Kilby, Clyde S., and Mead, Marjorie Lamp. *Brothers and Friends: The Diaries of Major Warren Hamilton Lewis.* San Francisco: HarperSanFrancisco, 1982.

Lewis, Warren H. (ed.). *The Lewis Papers: The Memoirs of the Lewis Family, 1850–1930.* 11 vols. Oxford, U.K.: Leeborough Press, 1933. Unpublished bound papers, Marion E. Wade Center, Wheaton College, Wheaton, Illinois, and the Bodleian Library, Oxford.

Miller, Ryder W. (ed.). *From Narnia to a Space Odyssey: The War of Ideas Between Arthur C. Clarke and C. S. Lewis.* New York: Simon & Schuster, 2003.

Sayer, George. *Jack: C. S. Lewis and His Times.* San Francisco: Harper-SanFrancisco, 1988.

Schofield, Stephen (ed.). *In Search of C. S. Lewis.* South Plainfield, N.J.: Bridge, 1983.

Starr, Nathan Comfort. "C. S. Lewis: A Personal Memoir." *Unicorn,* Spring 1972, *2*(2), 9–11.

Vanauken, Sheldon. *A Severe Mercy.* New York: HarperCollins, 1977.

Wilson, A. N. *C. S. Lewis: A Biography.* New York: Norton, 1990.

General Studies of Lewis and His Fiction

Adey, Lionel. *C. S. Lewis: Writer, Dreamer, and Mentor.* Grand Rapids, Mich.: Eerdmans, 1998.

Arnott, Anne. *The Secret Country of C. S. Lewis.* London: Hodder and Stoughton, 1974.

Campbell, David C., and Hess, Dale E. "Olympian Detachment: A Critical Look at the World of C. S. Lewis's Characters." *Studies in the Literary Imagination,* Fall 1989, *22,* 129–148.

Carnell, Corbin Scott. *Bright Shadow of Reality: C. S. Lewis and the Feeling Intellect.* Grand Rapids, Mich.: Eerdmans, 1974.

Christopher, Joe R. *C. S. Lewis.* Boston: Twayne, 1987.

Como, James. *Branches to Heaven: The Geniuses of C. S. Lewis.* Dallas: Spence, 1998.

Downing, David C. *Planets in Peril: A Critical Study of C. S. Lewis's Ransom Trilogy.* Amherst: University of Massachusetts Press, 1992.

Downing, David C. *Into the Region of Awe: Mysticism in C. S. Lewis.* Downers Grove, Ill.: InterVarsity Press, 2005.

Edwards, Bruce L. (ed.). *The Taste of the Pineapple: Essays on C. S. Lewis as Reader, Critic, and Imaginative Writer.* Bowling Green, Ohio: Bowling Green State University Popular Press, 1988.

Filmer, Kath. "The Polemic Image: The Role of Metaphor and Symbol in the Fiction of C. S. Lewis." *Seven: An Anglo-American Literary Review,* 1986, 7, 61–76.

Filmer, Kath. *The Fiction of C. S. Lewis: Mask and Mirror.* New York: St. Martin's Press, 1993.

Fuller, Edmund. *Books with Men Behind Them.* New York: Random House, 1962.

Gibson, Evan K. *C. S. Lewis: Spinner of Tales: A Guide to His Fiction.* Washington, D.C.: Christian University Press, 1980.

Glover, Donald E. *C. S. Lewis and the Art of Enchantment.* Athens: Ohio University Press, 1981.

González, Margarita Carretero, and Tenorio, Encarnación Hidalgo (eds.). *Behind the Veil of Familiarity: C. S. Lewis (1898–1998).* Bern, Switzerland: Peter Lang, 2001.

Green, Roger Lancelyn. *C. S. Lewis.* London: Bodley Head, 1963.

Hannay, Margaret Patterson. *C. S. Lewis.* New York: Ungar Books, 1981.

Hart, Dabney Adams. *Through the Open Door: A New Look at C. S. Lewis.* Tuscaloosa: University of Alabama Press, 1984.

Hillegas, Mark R. (ed.). *Shadows of Imagination: The Fantasies of C. S. Lewis, J. R. R. Tolkien, and Charles Williams.* Carbondale: Southern Illinois University Press, 1969.

Holbrook, David. *The Skeleton in the Wardrobe: C. S. Lewis's Fantasies.* Lewisburg, Pa.: Bucknell University Press, 1991.

Holmer, Paul L. *C. S. Lewis: The Shape of His Faith and Thought.* New York: HarperCollins, 1976.

Hooper, Walter. *C. S. Lewis: A Companion and Guide.* San Francisco: HarperSanFrancisco, 1996.

Howard, Thomas. *The Achievement of C. S. Lewis: A Reading of His Fiction.* Wheaton, Ill.: Harold Shaw, 1980.

Kilby, Clyde S. *Images of Salvation in the Fiction of C. S. Lewis.* Wheaton, Ill.: Harold Shaw, 1978.

Kort, Wesley A. *C. S. Lewis Then and Now.* Oxford, U.K.: Oxford University Press, 2001.

Kreeft, Peter. *C. S. Lewis: A Critical Essay.* Grand Rapids, Mich.: Eerdmans, 1969.

Kuhn, Daniel K. "The Joy of the Absolute: A Comparative Study of the Romantic Visions of William Wordsworth and C. S. Lewis." In Charles A. Huttar (ed.), *Imagination and the Spirit: Essays in Literature and the Christian Faith Presented to Clyde S. Kilby.* Grand Rapids, Mich.: Eerdmans, 1971.

Lindskoog, Kathryn. *C. S. Lewis: Mere Christian.* Downers Grove, Ill.: InterVarsity Press, 1981.

Manlove, Colin N. *C. S. Lewis: His Literary Achievement.* New York: St. Martin's Press, 1987.

Manlove, Colin N. "The Birth of a Fantastic World: C. S. Lewis's *The Magician's Nephew.*" *Journal of the Fantastic in the Arts,* 1988, *1*, 71–84.

Markos, Louis. *Lewis Agonistes.* Nashville, Tenn.: Broadman and Holman, 2003.

Masterman, Margaret. "C. S. Lewis: The Author and the Hero." *Twentieth Century,* Dec. 1955, *158*, 539–548.

Meilaender, Gilbert. *The Taste for the Other: The Social and Ethical Thought of C. S. Lewis.* Grand Rapids, Mich.: Eerdmans, 1978.

Mills, David (ed.). *The Pilgrim's Guide: C. S. Lewis and the Art of Witness.* Grand Rapids, Mich.: Eerdmans, 1998.

Moorman, Charles. *The Precincts of Felicity: The Augustinian City of the Oxford Christians.* Gainesville: University of Florida Press, 1966.

Murphy, Brian. "Enchanted Romanticism: The Legacy of C. S. Lewis." *Christianity and Literature,* Winter 1976, *25,* 13–26.

Murphy, Brian. *C. S. Lewis.* Mercer Island, Wash.: Starmont House, 1983.

Myers, Doris T. *C. S. Lewis in Context.* Kent, Ohio: Kent State University Press, 1994.

Norwood, W. D., Jr. "The Neo-Medieval Novels of C. S. Lewis." Unpublished doctoral dissertation, University of Texas, Austin, 1965.

Peters, John. *C. S. Lewis: The Man and His Achievement.* Exeter, U.K.: Pater Noster Press, 1985.

Purtill, Richard. *Lord of Elves and Eldils: Fantasy and Philosophy in C. S. Lewis and J. R. R. Tolkien.* Grand Rapids, Mich.: Zondervan, 1974.

Reilly, R. J. *Romantic Religion: A Study of Barfield, Lewis, Williams, and Tolkien.* Athens: University of Georgia Press, 1972.

Robson, W. W. "C. S. Lewis." *Cambridge Quarterly,* 1966, *1,* 252–272.

Rossi, Lee D. *The Politics of Fantasy: C. S. Lewis and J. R. R. Tolkien.* Ann Arbor, Mich.: UMI Research Press, 1984.

Schakel, Peter J. (ed.). *The Longing for a Form: Essays on the Fiction of C. S. Lewis.* Kent, Ohio: Kent State University Press, 1977.

Schakel, Peter J. "The Satiric Imagination of C. S. Lewis." *Studies in the Literary Imagination,* Fall 1989, *22,* 129–148.

Schakel, Peter J., and Huttar, Charles A. (eds.). *Word and Story in C. S. Lewis.* Columbia: University of Missouri Press, 1991.

Smith, Robert Houston. *Patches of Godlight: The Pattern of Thought in C. S. Lewis.* Athens: University of Georgia Press, 1981.

Spivak, Charlotte. "Images of Spirit in the Fiction of C. S. Lewis." *Mythlore,* 1987, *52,* 32–38.

Urang, Gunnar. *Shadows of Heaven: Religion and Fantasy in the Writing of C. S. Lewis, Charles Williams, and J.R.R. Tolkien.* Philadelphia: Pilgrim Press, 1971.

Walker, Andrew, and Patrick, James (eds.). *A Christian for All Christians: Essays in Honor of C. S. Lewis.* Washington, D.C.: Regnery Gateway, 1992.

Walsh, Chad. *C. S. Lewis: Apostle to the Skeptics.* New York: Macmillan, 1949.

Walsh, Chad. *The Literary Legacy of C. S. Lewis.* New York: Harcourt Brace Jovanovich, 1979.

Walsh, Chad. "C. S. Lewis: Critic, Creator, and Cult Figure." *Seven: An Anglo-American Literary Review,* 1981, *2,* 66–80.

Weatherby, H. L. "Two Medievalists: Lewis and Eliot on Christianity and Literature." *Sewanee Review,* Spring 1970, *78,* 330–347.

White, Luther William. *The Image of Man in C. S. Lewis.* Nashville, Tenn.: Abingdon Press, 1969.

Willis, John Randolph. *Pleasures Forevermore: The Theology of C. S. Lewis.* Chicago: Loyola University Press, 1983.

Wright, Marjorie Evelyn. "The Vision of the Cosmic Order in the Oxford Mythmakers." In Charles A. Huttar (ed.), *Imagination and the Spirit: Essays in Literature and the Christian Faith Presented to Clyde S. Kilby.* Grand Rapids, Mich.: Eerdmans, 1971.

Studies on the Chronicles of Narnia

Cox, John C. "Epistemological Release in *The Silver Chair.*" In Peter J. Schakel (ed.), *The Longing for a Form: Essays on the Fiction of C. S. Lewis.* Kent, Ohio: Kent State University Press, 1977.

Duriez, Colin. *A Field Guide to Narnia.* Downers Grove, Ill.: InterVarsity, 2004.

Edwards, Sarah Dudley. "The Theological Dimensions of the Narnia Stories." *Chesterton Review,* Oct./Nov. 1991, *17*(3–4), 429–435.

Ford, Paul F. *Companion to Narnia.* San Francisco: HarperSanFrancisco, 1980.

Hooper, Walter. "Preface." In Kathryn Lindskoog, *The Lion of Judah in Never-Never Land: The Theology of C. S. Lewis Expressed in His Fantasies for Children*. Grand Rapids, Mich.: Eerdmans, 1973.

Hooper, Walter. "Narnia: The Author, the Critics, and the Tale." In Peter J. Schakel (ed.), *The Longing for a Form: Essays on the Fiction of C. S. Lewis*. Kent, Ohio: Kent State University Press, 1977.

Hooper, Walter. *Past Watchful Dragons: The Narnian Chronicles of C. S. Lewis*. New York: Collier Books, 1979.

Huttar, Charles A. "C. S. Lewis's Narnia and the 'Grand Design.'" In Peter J. Schakel (ed.), *The Longing for a Form: Essays on the Fiction of C. S. Lewis*. Kent, Ohio: Kent State University Press, 1977.

Karkainen, Paul. *Narnia Explored*. Old Tappan, N.J.: Revell, 1979.

Lindskoog, Kathryn. *The Lion of Judah in Never-Never Land: The Theology of C. S. Lewis Expressed in His Fantasies for Children*. Grand Rapids, Mich.: Eerdmans, 1973.

Lindskoog, Kathryn. *Journey into Narnia*. Pasadena, Calif.: Hope, 1998.

Manlove, Colin N. "The Birth of a Fantastic World: C. S. Lewis's *The Magician's Nephew*." *Journal of the Fantastic in the Arts*, 1988, *1*, 71–84.

Manlove, Colin N. *The Chronicles of Narnia: The Patterning of a Fantastic World*. New York: Twayne, 1993.

Montgomery, John Warwick. "The Chronicles of Narnia and the Adolescent Reader." In John Warwick Montgomery (ed.), *Myth, Allegory, and Gospel*. Minneapolis, Minn.: Bethany, 1974.

Murrin, Michael. "The Multiple Worlds of the Narnia Stories." In Peter J. Schakel and Charles A. Huttar (eds.), *Word and Story in C. S. Lewis*. Columbia: University of Missouri Press, 1991.

Myers, Doris T. "The Anglican: Spiritual Style in the Narnia Chronicles." In David Mills (ed.), *The Pilgrim's Guide: C. S. Lewis and the Art of Witness*. Grand Rapids, Mich.: Eerdmans, 1998.

Sammons, Martha C. *A Guide Through Narnia*. Wheaton, Ill.: Harold Shaw, 1979.

Schakel, Peter J. *Reading with the Heart: The Way into Narnia.* Grand Rapids, Mich.: Eerdmans, 1979.

Schakel, Peter J. "Elusive Birds and Narrative Nets: The Appeal of Story in C. S. Lewis' Chronicles of Narnia." In Andrew Walker and James Patrick (eds.), *A Christian for All Christians: Essays in Honor of C. S. Lewis.* Washington, D.C.: Regnery Gateway, 1992.

Schakel, Peter J. "Imagination and the Arts." In *C. S. Lewis: Journeying to Narnia and Other Worlds.* Columbia: University of Missouri Press, 2002.

Shulevitz, Judith. "Don't Mess with Aslan." *New York Times Book Review,* Aug. 26, 2001, p. 27.

Smith, Stephen M. "Awakening from the Enchantment of Worldliness: The Chronicles of Narnia as Pre-Apologetics." In David Mills, (ed.), *The Pilgrim's Guide: C. S. Lewis and the Art of Witness.* Grand Rapids, Mich.: Eerdmans, 1998.

Taliaferro, Charles. "A Narnian Theory of Atonement." *Scottish Journal of Theology,* 1988, *41,* 75–92.

Tixier, Elaine. "Imagination Baptized, or 'Holiness' in the Chronicles of Narnia." In Peter J. Schakel (ed.), *The Longing for a Form: Essays on the Fiction of C. S. Lewis.* Kent, Ohio: Kent State University Press, 1977.

Ward, Michael. "Through the Wardrobe: A Famous Image Explored." *Seven: An Anglo-American Review,* 1998, *15,* 55–71.

ACKNOWLEDGMENTS

I would like to thank first my editor at Jossey-Bass, Julianna Gustafson (spelled *Jewelianna* in Narnian), for encouraging me to undertake this project and for offering insightful and tactful advice as it developed. Thank you as well to my agent, Giles Anderson, for his usual efficiency, professionalism, and cordial assistance.

I am grateful to Wayne Martindale of Wheaton College for providing me with the benefit of his expertise. My thanks also to the leaders and staff of the Marion E. Wade Center at Wheaton, especially Christopher J. Mitchell and Marjorie L. Mead, for the many ways in which they have assisted me and so many other visiting scholars.

My colleagues at Elizabethtown College have been generous and supportive throughout the writing process. I am especially obliged to Dana Mead, the English department's specialist in children's literature, and to Kevin Scott, our specialist in English education. My editorial assistant, Anne Baublitz, also merits commendation for her thoughtful and careful work.

I count myself fortunate that members of my own family are not only among my most sympathetic readers, but also among the most perceptive. Thanks especially to my brother Don and my wife, Crystal, for numerous valuable suggestions on clarity and readability.

I would also like to recognize the distinguished work of several individuals at Jossey-Bass, including Andrea Flint, the production editor, and Paula Goldstein, the senior art director who produced the book cover in collaboration with the Design Works Group. I am grateful as well to Sandy Seigle, the marketing manager, Carolyn Uno, the copyeditor, and to Richard Sheppard, who rendered the page illustrations. I set out to make *Into the Wardrobe* a useful and readable book; thank you to all those at Jossey-Bass who helped turn it into a beautiful book.

THE AUTHOR

David C. Downing is a leading C. S. Lewis expert, award-winning author, and professor of English at Elizabethtown College in Lancaster County, Pennsylvania. His articles about Lewis have appeared in such publications as *Christianity Today, Christianity and Literature, Books & Culture, Christian Scholars Review,* and numerous other journals. His books include *Planets in Peril,* about the Space Trilogy; *The Most Reluctant Convert,* a biography of Lewis that was named one of the Top Ten Religion Books of the Year by the American Library Association; and *Into the Region of Awe,* a study of the mystical elements in Lewis's life and writings.

INDEX

H

Moral education, key element
of, 91

Moral equilibrium, 105

Moral failure and recovery, illustrating, 90

Moral growth, 96

Moral health: discerning, clearest way of, 100; requisite for,
96

Moral laws, universal and unalterable, 90–91

Moral momentum, 93

Moral of a story, the, issue of,
105–106

Moral psychology, discussion of,
89–106

Moral qualities, early clue to a
character's, 133

Moral regeneration, 100,
101–102, 103

Moral relativism, 91

Morality, Christian, 83–84

Morgan le Fay, 164

Morris, W., 46, 59, 116

Morte D'Arthur (Malory), 115

Moses, 172

Mother of C. S. Lewis. *See*
Lewis, F. H.

Mullugutherum, 138

Multicolored bird in the apple
tree, defined, 165

"My Little Man," 165

"My son, my son," 165

Mysterious workings, term associated with, 121, 122, 123

Mythology, 15–16, 19, 34, 52,
55, 109, 139, 141, 142, 166,
168, 170

Myths: associating paganism
with, 109; classical,
109–110; of the dying god,
19, 34; love of, 74; true, 19,
52

N

Naiads, 74, 165

Names: as allusions, 131–135;
of children, 142–146; choos-
ing, based on sound,
136–138; from classical languages, 135–136; common-
place, warning against, 129;
of evil beings, 141–142; fascination for, 129–131; nine,
of Aslan, 171; of other Talking Beasts, 138–140. *See also
specific names*

Narnia: arrival of Pevensie children in, 89; bringing evil
into, 97; called into, 121;
creation of, 73; dark void of,
Aslan filling, 73; the fall taking place before creation in,
74; first king of, 114; gateway into, 35; goal of reaching, and the North, 48;
industrializing, thoughts of,
98, 99; last days of, 54, 55,
126; name of, meaning of,
131; new, 82; origins of,
writing about, 36, 38; plot to
invade, 49; protection of,
Digory placing, over his own
desires, 76; pulled back into,
40; reliable guides in, 89–90;
return to, 104; safety of,